AF539873

INDUSTRIAL MANAGEMENT

DPH Management Series

INDUSTRIAL MANAGEMENT

J M DEWAN • K N SUDARSHAN

DISCOVERY PUBLISHING HOUSE
NEW DELHI-110002

Discovery Publishing House
4831/24, Ansari Road, Darya Ganj
New Delhi - 110 002 (INDIA)

Industrial Management
©1996, Editors
Reprinted-2011

ISBN-81-7141-363-3

PRINTED IN INDIA

Printed at Mehra Offset Press, Delhi

Preface

The management world is in transition. The causes of this transition are many, but the major one is the vast changes in knowledge and in the information that flows in and out of organizations. This changing information disrupts traditions, established processes, well-known procedures, and routine ways of doing things. New principles, concepts, techniques, ideas, expressions, processes, and procedures are emerging, moving us to a new plateau of professional practice. Trying to capture this changing knowledge and information is like trying to capture the atmosphere. How can you do it when the atmosphere is continually shifting and when you need the atmosphere to do the capturing? The best we can do is find a peak from which we can at least get a perspective on management as a whole, decide on the work and responsibilities of management, and gather in whatever practical management information we can. A team of experts in this series represent some of the best contemporary thinking and information available. They represent many major successful corporations, active consulting agencies, and well-known educational institutions, and all are experts on what is happening with the flow of knowledge and information in the management world. This is a lofty pinnacle from which to survey the management world.

Managers and supervisors clamor for current information and guidelines to help solve formidable problems in their work world—problems that range from "how to do it" to "how to resolve conflict when doing it." Many problems are generated from miscommunication and incompetence. As the management practice proceeds from the complex to the supercomplex, problem solving becomes a large-scale challenge requiring new knowledge and skills. Managers and supervisors cannot wait for research breakthroughs with real-world answers to solve these dilemmas. They must tackle them here and now with the useful information and proven practices immediately available. Whether making a decision, solving a problem setting up a procedure, designing a process, or resolving a behaviour conflict, a manager must rely heavily on information. To a great extent, management practitioners are information workers; that is, they generate, distribute, store, retrieve, and consume information. Competence in finding and using the right information at the needed time determines to a considerable extent competence in the management function, activity, or responsibility. The *DPH Management Series* attempts to fill this need for usable information in spite of the changing nature of its subject.

The *DPH Management Series* not a book to be read and later discarded. It is a reference book, a tool to be used by managerial personnel in the day-to-day work of an organization. Like a tool, it should never be more than a reach away when a new situation emerges that demands its use. This series aim to achieve a first-and practical and proven knowledge and information as a self-development opportunity for those who are moving into or upward in management. A complete spectrum of management subjects is immediately available for orientation, study, analysis, assimilation, and problem solving. Within one set of covers is the view of management as a totality. The management field is loaded with ideas that the organization of this handbook series unique logic. It follows both levels and areas of responsibilities of an organization.

The work of this handbook series is the collaborative effort of many outstanding people in the management field. The motivation for this work varied from individual to individual, but the central motivation that united us all was the excitement of capturing the management state-of-the-art and sharing it with colleagues in the dynamic profession of management.

This series should be of great help to managerial practitioners at any organizational level who are responsible for a function, department, or set of responsibilities. The handbook series will also give these practitioners insights into management roles and approaches in other areas as well. The subject matter encompasses top, middle, and lower management. Special emphasis was placed on managing people, time, space, budgets, and resources to give the handbook extra utility for middle and lower management. Students of management in university or educational institutions will find the series an invaluable resource for adding "real world" practices to their academic and theoretical foundations. MBA students will gain an invaluable overview of the total organization to complement their MBA degree. Administrators and public managers can become acquainted with practices employed by managers and supervisors in private organizations. These practices are not always directly applicable in public sector bodies, but with thought and modifications, these private practices can adapt to public organizations. Public and university librarians will find the handbook an indispensable reference for the multitude of questions on many topics from the general public, special groups, associations, and students.

Editors

Contents

1 Industrial Conflict

The conflict is basic to industrial relations is a proposition echoed by scholars of diverse disciplinary backgrounds and normative conviction. The systems analyst views it as ubiquitous, but ultimately as a form of deviant behavior, and hence focuses upon rule-making processes for tension management and grievance resolution. Pluralists and Marxists see it as endemic in industrial societies with substantial private sectors (the former stress interest-group divisions and the latter the cleavages based on social class). And most would concur with Faucheux and Rojot that 'conflict is the motive force of the industrial relations system', since its various processes are essentially designed to contain labour unrest. To commence the account of comparative themes with industrial conflict is thus scarcely contentious and involves an explanation of strike patterns and a number of other forms of worker protest.

A theory of industrial conflict

The heterogeneous conflict strategies of employers and managers, labour and trade unions, and governments and members of the state are formed within instrumental or value rationality that encourage a series of high or low dispute outcomes. These are reflected in conspicuous variations in the incidence of strikes amongst nations and, above all, in distinctive profiles or 'shapes' of stoppages, characterized by the dominance of duration, breadth or frequency.

The meanings which inform given strategies are linked first of all with culture, which affects a number of qualitative dimensions of strike activity, even though, except in the Third World, its consequences for quantitative aspects of disputes are more circumscribed. The influence of ideology is difficult to disentangle from broader political conditions, but the strategy of 'mobilization'is connected with radical or revolutionary movements and with strikes of unusual breadth.

So far as constraints on strategic choices are concerned, different political systems are associated with the relative emphasis on organized or unorganized conflicts respectively, Political 'exchanges' between organized labour and governments explain low levels of conflict in a number of countries. Moreover, in their absence, the strike is widely deployed as a form of political protest (especially where there are strong Communist Party-trade union ties). However, since the Second World War, a series of economic conditions such as movements in real wages, unemployment and inflation have been at the heart of strike activity in the west. These not only account for a number of variations amongst countries at a given point in time, but also the longer-term movements (notably the main cycles of conflict).

At an intermediary level of analysis, the organizational strategies of management designed to secure job control are consistent with strikes of long duration. Furthermore, amongst institutional variables, the degree of consolidation of collective bargaining agreements underlies dispute profiles dominated by frequency of stoppage. A long duration of disputes is also associated with the constitutional nature of strikes, the level of bargaining, long-term contracts, legally (or morally) binding no-strike agreements and the scope of issues covered by collective bargaining. Finally, the distribution of power amongst the 'actors' largely explains which conflict strategies are ascendant at any given moment in time. And, above all, in eastern Europe, the pervasiveness of the state ensures that conflict is predominantly unorganized (even though recent relative trade union autonomy has resulted in higher strike propensities).

Conflict strategies

Notwithstanding a common interest amongst the parties in ensuring that the wealth of a nation is not undermined completely by internecine strife, conflicts in industry occur in both the production and the distribution spheres. But whether or not these deeply rooted, latent tensions become manifest in strike activity and other forms of discontent reflects the diverse strategic choices of all the 'actors' set within wider meanings and constraints.

Conflict strategies are interpretable through distinctive orientations associated with instrumental and value rationality respectively. Taking employers and managers first of all, an overriding commitment to profitability, productivity and economic performance or the defence of private enterprise against militant trade unionism can be expected to produce a high incidence of disputes (a priority for human relations policies or for benevolent paternalism being usually accompanied by industrial peace). In the case of labour and the trade unions, conflict stems either from its perceived tactical advantage for securing improvements in pay and conditions or from its connection with policies of political mobilization and radical societal transformation. Discord is less probable, however, if instrumental goals can be achieved through established institutional channels or there is a political commitment to maintaining, say a 'Sympathetic' party in office. For governments and members of the state, policies which centre on economic criteria for 'System' performance, or which seek to secure the dominance of given political creeds (regardless of the implications for social order), will generate industrial unrest. Conversely, an emphasis on the social accomplishments of a society or on wider citizenship strategies rooted in industrial democracy and high welfare spending can be presumed to advance harmony.

Strategies and industrial conflict: outcomes

To be sure, the choices outlined so far and their outcomes are set within broader meanings and are constrained in practice, no least by the distribution of power. But the upshot is an intricate and diversified pattern of industrial conflict amongst nations. moreover, although, for analytical purposes, our focus will be largely on strike activity, at the outset the many aspects of conflict should be affirmed through the trenchant statement of Clark Keer:

> The manifestation of hostility is confined to no single outlet. its means of expression are as unlimited as the ingenuity of man. The strike is the most common and most visible expression. But conflict with the employer may also take the form of peaceful bargaining and grievance handling, of boycotts, of political action, of restriction of output, of sabotage, of absenteeism, or of personnel turnover. Several of these forms, such as sabotage, restriction of output, absenteeism and turnover, may take place on an individual as well as on an organised basis and constitute alternatives to collective action. Even the strike itself is of many varieties. It may take the form of refusal to work overtime or to perform a certain process. It may even involve such rigid adherence to the rules that output is stifled.

Moreover, strikes themselves are not homogeneous events. Rather, as Gouldner has observed, they involve a cessation of work, a breakdown in the flow of consent and an open expression of 'aggression' and remain 'a social phenomenon of enormous complexity, which, in its totally, is never susceptible to complete description, let alone complete explanation. Indeed, leaving aside problems of validity and reliability of data. The experience of particular countries is by no means consistent on every measure of strike activity. The disparate measures of strikes used in comparative analysis yield four main dimensions: (1) frequency- the number of work stoppages in a given unit of analysis over a specified time period; (2) breadth - the number of workers who participate in work stoppages; (3) duration - the length of stoppages, usually in man-days lost through stoppages. And, as Table 6.2 reveals, these are typically measured in terms of: (1) number of stoppages per 100,000 wage and salary earners; (2) involvement per 1,000 wage and salary earners. of working days lost per 1,000 wage and salary earners. Moverover, although great caution is required in their interpretation and use, if the USA is taken as an example, fairly low scores in terms of frequency and breadth of stoppage sharply contrast with an unusually high average duration of disputes and a figure close to the median for impact.

Diversity in strike activity reflects varied strategies of the 'actors' and also the specific functions of strikes, which are reveled in pronounced differences amongst countries in dispute profiles or 'shapes'. On this basis, it will be noted that five main types of strike pattern for leading 'western' countries are discernible, with he fundamental contrasts between the United States, Italy and Australia being especially worthy of attention. These are:

Type 1: Long duration of stoppages is dominant: characteristic of the United States of America, Canada and Ireland.

Type 2: Considerable breadth of disputes largely determines overall 'shape': exemplified by Italy and, to a lesser extent, Finland, Spain and Isral.

Type 3: The structure of strikes is determined principally by the relatively high frequency figures: the case of Australia and New Zealand and, to a lesser extent, France and Portugal.

Type 4: A similar ranking in terms of frequency, duration and membership involvement produces the characteristic strike 'shape' of the United Kingdom and Japan.

Type 5: A typically low incidence of strike activity, but the duration of the few stoppages is not insignificant: characteristic of Belgium, Denmark, Netherlands, Norway and Sweden.

Patterns of industrial conflict: meanings and constraints

But to avoid and excessively 'voluntaristic' analysis of industrial conflict it is vital to take account of various meanings and constraints.

Meanings, culture and ideology

The pervasiveness of broad meanings in the interpretation of strikes is evident first of all in the consequences of culture for variations in qualitative aspects of disputes. For illustration, the Organization for Economic Cooperation and Development has suggested that, in respect of Japan, there are three unusual constituents of strikes: the societal pressure towards consensus which places a 'heavy responsibility' on the parties to resolve disputes 'without resort to overt conflict'; the tendency for industrial action to take a demonstrative form (e.g.vacations being taken en masse, banning overtime, pasting posters or 'wearing head or armbands bearing the unsatisfied demands); and the preference of the unions for 'harassment' rather than 'damage' because of their close structural ties with the enterprise.

To be sure, the more specific effects of culture on quantitative diversity are more contentious in the west, the case here being usually advanced by way of a rather superficial contrast between northern and Latin European countries. For example, Faucheux and Rojot have proposed that the assertion of individualism (reflecting Protestant rather than Catholic values) militates against collective forms of action and hence strike activity and, in turn, accounts for the lower strike propensities in, say, Scandinavia rather than in Italy and Spain. Against this, however, in studies in which culture has been measured. Sweden and Norway have been found to be more 'collectivist' than countries like the USA in which strike activity is far more common. Typically, too, the density of unionization (also reflecting collectivism) is much higher in northern than in Latin Europe. And, as we shall see later, the major historical shifts in pattern are almost impossible to explain on the basis of cultural traits.

But there is evidence to suggest that variations in strikes in the Third World are related to cultural differences since the neo-Confucian countries are characterized by emphasis on harmony of interests and are virtually free of stoppages. To assess the experience of developing countries, data are available in the International Labour Office's Yearbook of Labour Statistics, but questions remain over comparability, and essential material on employment (particularly on wage and salary earners) is incomplete and subject to considerable error. However, using the measure of working days lost as the least vulnerable to problems of reliability and validity, indications are that in far Eastern countries strikes have only a limited impact. By contrast, a lowmoderate incidence of disputes occurs in most African countries (although the sample here is both selected and small); while India and a number of Latin American and Carbbean countries are unusually strike-prone. But, although fundamental, cultural is not the sole explanation for these disparities. Other factors include the historical circumstances surrounding the rise of organized labour (particularly its part in colonial struggles) and the organizational and institutional structure of trade unions themselves.

The effects of ideologies are difficult to disentangle from those of political systems, but there are strong grounds for concluding that they are closely entwined with strike 'shapes' and especially those dominated by breadth of stoppage. For example, in his comparative studies of France and the UK, Gallie has established that, by contrast with their British countrierparts, French trade unionists are more committed to 'mobilization' than to 'representation' and have more combative, politically conscious and oppositional orientations corresponding to radical and revolutionary ideologies. Moreover, while the overall strike rate is not decisively higher on every measure in France than in Britain, the varying profiles can be readily interpreted by ideological diversity. Indeed, even allowing for dissimilar recording methods, varied objectives of labour are clearly reflected in the breadth and frequency of strikes in France by comparison with Britain, where disputes are typically of longer duration and have a noticeable economic impact. In general, too, although wider political elements are also relevant, the mobilization strategy of trade union leaders in Italy are indelibly imprinted on the national strike 'profile'.

Constraints

Political conditions

But a comprehensive explanation for variations in strike activity amongst nations has to encompass the constraints of environment, organization, institution and th distribution of power. Indeed, the political systems of individual countries, the 'exchanges' between organized labour and governments and the relationship between Communist parties and trade unions are all relevant here.

The effects of political system will be examined in more detail in connection with the role of the state in eastern Europe, but it is worth mentioning that integrative one-party regimes tend to reduce the level of organized conflict at the expense of appreciable problems of spontaneous workers' actions, including job changing, absenteeism and occasionally more violent uprising. However, in the west, the adoption of strategic 'political exchanges' is basic to the explanation of the relatively strike-free character of some countries. Indeed, successful institutionalization of conflict depends in large measure on labour abandoning strike action in return for full participation in the national polity and a just distribution of economic rewards, accomplished through appreciable levels of welfare-state spending Korpi and Shalev. By contrast, where strike activity remains high disputes typically retain their significance as instruments of political action which are designed to compel government intervention in disputes, to impress on public consciousness the force and vigour behind workers' demands and 'to exact political pressure on the centre.

The political 'exchange' thesis applied well to long-term movements in patterns of strike activity in the west in general up until the Second World War and to the north and central European experience thereafter. At risk of oversimplification, during the first half of the twentieth century, there were parallel movements in strike activity in all these countries. The growth of unions and working-class political action resulted in a mobilization that 'generated everywhere a great wave of strike activity', which, in the words of Shorter and Tilly, produced with similar modes of worker representation in the central immediate post-war period, the 'fundamental identity; or strike activity gave rise to major divergencies. The first comprised the west European pattern of Italy and France of strikes of great size and brevity reflecting the determination of 'the politically impotent working classes' to participate in national politics. The second was the post-war north European pattern of Scandinavia the netherlands and West Germany in which the strike largely withered away following the entry of the working classes into the polity through the political success of the Social Democratic or labour parties. Ad the third was the North American pattern, in which significant levels of industrial conflict remained but the 'strike shape' was dissimilar from that of western Europe.

Taking the cast of Sweden, a dramatic alternation in strike proneness closely followed the accession to power of the Social Democratic Party in 1932, an event which encouraged labour first to defer and then to abandon its earlier strategy of wholesale industrial militancy. In other words, 'The primary cause of the record low level of industrial disputes in Sweden in the post-war decades' was the shift in power distribution in the society and 'the changes in the conflict strategies of the parties which this induced. Moreover, in countries where the strike remains a primary weapon of working -class political action, frequent and broad-based stoppages predominate.

In some countries without successful institutionalization of industrial conflict, the situation is compounded by the relationship between dominant Communist parties and trade unions for, in these circumstances, disputes retain their significance as a form of political action and this has ramifications for both overall strike propensity and the shape of stoppages. Hibbs has thus shown that 'strike activity varies with the relative size of Communist party membership', and this further endorses the proposition 'that Communist parties in advanced industrial societies remain important agencies for the mobilization of latent discontent and the crystallisation of labour-capital cleavages'. For instance, a high incidence of dispute in countries such as Italy is attributable in part to the presence of a strong Communist party with links with the leading trade union. Moreover, the

Italian strike profile, with relatively large, brief and frequent stoppages, reflects the dominance of socalled 'Leninist' trade union organization principles with fairly small memberships and slender financial resources.

Economic conditions

For much of the post-war period, however, economic conditions have been more elemental than political exchanges to the explanation of varying strike activity amongst western nations. Hence, in a three-country comparison of France, Italy an the SUS, Snyder showed that the political model was a significant predictor of the frequency and size of conflict in all countries up until the Second World War. In the post-war years, however, on account of a greater success in institutionalizing industrial conflict, economic rather than political forces became dominant.

The main variations in strike patterns since the Second World War are set out in which cover, respectively, changing patterns of: (1) involvement and duration; and (2) the number and impact of stoppages. The first reveals divergent movements in Italy and France, the northern European countries, North America and Belgium, Denmark and the UK. The second highlights further complexities associated with the wave of disputes which swept across most western nations in the late 1960s and early 1970s. It also shows that while the number of stoppages increased after the mid-1970s in North America, Australasia, Japan, Finland, France and Italy, there was no similar acceleration in the Netherlands, Norway, Switzerland and the UK. In the same period, the impact of disputes became more severe in Australia and New Zealand, Italy, France, Canada, ireland and the UK; but in the USA, Austria and Germany there was a more varied and fluctuating pattern.

The primary conditions underlying these complex movements are economic factors such as shifts in real wages and levels of unemployment. Hibbs thus showed that short-term fluctuations in strike activity in the leading western nations reflected a rational economic calculation and working-class sophistication in relation to movements in these economic variables. Real rather than money wages were critical because of their effect on the gap between the worker's level of aspiration for a particular standard of living and its actual achievement. And, although there is no constant relationship between these variables, allied with labour's attempt to 'capitalize on the strategic advantages of a tight labour market', an inverse association obtains for the volume of industrial conflict and the rate of unemployment.

Moreover, looking at the long-term changes in patterns of conflict, in conjunction with economic movements, there is strong support for a cyclical rather than linear interpretation. Ross and Hartman of course noted that a decline in strike activity and an alternation in dispute practices accompanies the integration of the working class into the political system. And, while the typical stoppages at the initial phases of industrialization were restricted in size and low in frequency, but long-drawn out the mid-twentieth-century pattern was one in which the size of strikes increased, stoppages became more frequent and in which each dispute was o 'markedly reduced duration'. More generally, too, those adopting the 'withering away of the strike' hypothesis identified three leading supporting conditions: the creation of a web of institutional rules, the institutional isolation of industrial conflict from political struggles, and improved material prosperity.

But the case for a long-term decline was effectively destroyed by the upsurge in disputes in western Europe in the late 1960s and early 1970s. Moreover, to explain the occurrence of strike waves, the strategies of 'actors' in a period of high inflation are paramount. Much of the unrest of the early 1970s was induced by government policies implemented to reverse an inflationary spiral. Increased conflict was in part a reflection of the growth of unofficial action, but it also represented the militant strategies of previously quiescent groups which had borne 'much of the brunt of the counter-inflation policies'. Specifically, a number of 'frustration factors' came into operation in the three-to-four-year period prior to the strikes: (1) Moderation of real wage growth, with a complementary reduction in labour's share and increase in the share of profits; (2) compression of differentials between skilled and semi-skilled workers and/or public and private sectors and/or different industries; and (3) rationalization of production, via mergers and/or increasing workloads and/or disadvantageous changes in plant payment structures'. The growing intervention of the state in overall economic planning, as well as more directly in industrial relations, also ensured that the institutional isolation of labour disputes was difficult to sustain. Finally, an inflationary background led to the disruption of established procedural and substantive norms and was reflected, most obviously, in the rise of plant-level bargaining and the multiplicity of overlapping negotiational units and levels.

Organizational strategies of management

But economic conditions can also impact on strike activity through the organizational strategies of employers. Above all, in highly competitive environments with pressure on product markets, managements pursue 'unitary' industrial relations strategies which are reflected in appreciable levels of intensity in the struggle for control. And the consequence is a high level of strike activity, together with a willingness of the parties to engage in long battles. Hence, if breadth of stoppage is rooted in the ideologies and strategies of labour, managerial policies and actions are firmly stamped on strike profiles characterized by long duration.

This so-called 'job control thesis' receives strong support from North America, where the conventional shape of disputes reflects extensive employer hostility to trade unions and to encroachments on managerial 'prerogatives', coupled with a willingness to carry through such convictions in actual behaviour. However, the case is only partially valid because, in the USA, 'business unionism', with a substantial dues-paying membership, enables labour to countenance 'trench warfare'. Moreover, in ireland, where there are a small number of extensive and protracted stoppages, managerial industrial relations strategies are more similar to the UK, which has a different strike profile, than to the USA. Indeed, the pattern in Eire is largely explicable through the pronounced tendency for the parties to interpret disputes in terms of conflicts about rights rather than interests, for this produces a limited number of very fundamental struggles which the processes of compromise and concession that typify collective bargaining are ill-adapted to resolve.

In sum, the thesis emphasizing managerial strategies for job control requires further validation to be strategies for job north American continent. yet it remains a valuable corrective to the one-sided focus on working-class and trade union behaviour of the 'political' school and it reinforces the case that explanations for strike activity are complex, not least because disputes have different meanings and functions in individual countries.

Industrial relations institutions

But the institutional structure of industrial relations is also both a significant explanation for overall strike propensity and a primary determinant of variations in strike 'shape. Not all the variables isolated here are of equal explanatory moment solidation of bargaining structure would thus appear to be especially critical) and most are, in their turn, rooted in deeper economic, political and social movements. But the institutional thesis is vital for understanding dispute profiles typified by high frequency of stoppage. The earlier proponents of this argument were Ross and hartman who, in addition to labour political activity traced variations in strike patterns amongst countries to the combined effects of organizational stability, leadership conflicts in the labour movement the status of union-management relations and the role of the state. Clegg has also identified a limited number of the dimensions of collective bargaining structure as decisive: 'plant bargaining leads to a relatively large number of official strikes' industry or regional bargaining is conducive 'to a smaller number of larger official strikes', while the number of strikes is also 'likely to be high where dispute procedures are absent or defective.

The degree of consolidation of bargaining structure correlates well with variations in strikes. Hibbs thus contrasted decentralized systems of collective bargaining with centralized systems and highly centralized systems and demonstrated a strong covariance between the mean level of strike activity nd the degree of centralization of bargaining systems. And, as Edwards has pointed out, there is a virtually automatic tendency for centralized systems to incorporate into one dispute what would otherwise be several separate strikes under plant bargaining and hence to reduce the overall number of stoppages.

Considerable caution is obviously necessary in comparisons of frequency but profiles in which it is dominant are explained not only by the prevalence of plant-level negotiations but also by the variable functions of strikes. For example, the large number of stoppages in Australia and France can be interpreted as brief demonstrations which put pressure on negotiators. Moreover in the USA and Canada, the prolonged duration of stoppages reflects: (1) the constitutional nature of disputes (2) the level of bargaining : (3) long-term contracts; (4) legally and morally binding no-strike clauses; and (5) the wide range of subjects covered in agreements.

However, other aspects of institutional structure, such as organizational stability and leadership conflicts, have only a restricted impact. Britain and the United States thus have comparatively mature labour movements but the strike clearly shows no sign of withering away in either of these countries. The impact of leadership conflicts is more difficult to assess but may be expected to apply to variations amongst t particular unions or industries rather than to country-by-country differences. For instance, as Edwards has pointed out in the United States, even the healing of the AFL-CIO rift had no appreciable affect on the strike pattern. Moreover, while the different modes of third-party intervention can be relevant, it is hard to demonstrate any direct links between, say, arbitration machinery and the overall incidence of conflict. Australia thus remains highly strike-prone despite the presence of the Federal Australian Conciliation and Arbitration Commission and its reinforcement through a series of State tribunals and wages boards.

The power of the 'actors'

The relative strength of the parties in the industrial relations system underlies a number of variations in industrial conflict, and, in particular, explains which conflict strategies become ascendant. Managerial strength permits strategies aimed at securing job control at the expense of 'constitutionalism', while labour weakness accounts for the dominance of breadth of stoppage in a given strike profile, reflecting 'demonstrative' acts of protest rather than the sustained pressure at the centre of a successful 'political exchanges'. But the effects of the distribution of power are best exemplified by eastern Europe, where a dominant role for the state ensures not only formally integrative functions for trade unions, but also that conflict is typically unorganized.

There is not systematic and reliable evidence on industrial conflict in the he Soviet Union or other countries in eastern Europe, but strikes and a wide range of unorganized forms of protest do occur. However, by comparison with the 'average' level for the west, organized conflict has almost certainly been reduced by a belief system in which homogeneity of interests and social harmony is emphasised' and by the 'lack of any tradition of unions organizing strikes to improve pay and conditions'. To be sure, disputes in the 1920s were a serious problem in the Soviet Union; so much so, indeed, that by 1929, Party leaders had 'declared strike action to be anti-proletarian and counterproductive'. Recently, too, strikes have occurred in Moscow, Leningrade, Baku Kaments-Podolshii, Temir-Tau and kaunas. Again, despite official denials, in 1980, for instance, there were reports of major work stoppages involving between 70,000 and 200,000 auto workers in Togliatti and Gorki. Nevertheless, while the data presented in TAble 6.6 unavoidably understate the total, there are probably no more than a 'few dozen' strikes per year in the USSR.

To explain the low incidence of organized conflict in the soviet Union and allied states, the official ideology and political-economic structure of centralized forms of socialism are relevant. But power relations within industry and the wider society are more fundamental. Indeed, an omnipresent state ensures that industrial disputes invariably have political implications and, because trade unions in most of eastern Europe still have integrative structures and functions, conflict is predominantly unorganized. In a valuable review of 'spontaneous' workers' activities in the Soviet Union, Pravda has thus listed four main types of behaviour which indicate dissatisfaction: job changing, lack of discipline, writing critical letter and collective protest. The most widespread form of action is job turnover which, following the removal of labour controls in 1956, has run at a rate between 19 and 22 per cent per annum.

Violation of work rules is also a 'serious form of workers' spontaneity' and involves the loss of 'tens of millions' of mandays annually. The writing of critical letters to the press is very common and, even in the Stalin era, received official approval. Again, despite problems of editorial selection and of identifying the correspondents, in a study of those who wrote letters to Komsomolskaya Pravda, workers were found to have penned more than any other complainants. Moreover, protest action itself is not confined to strikes, but is also reflected in appeals to higher authorities, public demonstrations and dissident activity. A common form of industrial action by Soviet workers is also to slow-down production. And finally, although these are rare, rioting and violence accompanying spontaneous uprisings do occur.

Indeed, to reinforce the link between the degree of autonomy and influence of trade unions and the likelihood of disputes taking an organized form, the case of Yugoslavia is instructive. In Chapter 4, we observed how trade unions there have become prominent and it is thus scarcely surprising that strikes have proliferated as a consequence. The first known strikes in Yugoslavia under socialism took place in 1958, but up to 1969 a further 1,900 work stoppages were recorded and from 1973 'more than 200 occurred in Slovenia alone'. Moreover, because of the widespread use of market mechanisms, as in the west, disputes have typically centred on distribution and production issues which arise in the actual enterprise rather than on, say, the price of consumer goods.

2 Industrial Democracy

A belief in the virtues of democratic control is anchored in fundamental human values which pervade most industrial societies. Widely advocated as a solution to alienation, for optimizing individual freedom in a collective context, and as a means of obviating the undesirable effects of asymmetrical distributions of power, it has captured the imagination of the reformer seeking to eradicate latent and machinery for industrial democracy is richly heterogeneous in type.

A theory of industrial democracy

Variability amongst nations is interpreted, first and foremost, as the outcome of strategic choices, focused in different preferences of the initiating actors; and patterned by broad cultural and ideological meanings, public policies and legislative enactments. Culture is reflected in cohesive national values, which have diverse consequences for institutional innovation in industrial democracy. Ideology is also critical to the experiences of nations, for the types of institution, their initiating agents and principal objectives diverge fundamentally on the basis of the precepts of modern capitalism, managerialism, corporatism, liberal pluralism and social democracy, democratic socialism, state socialism and syndicalism. Moreover, at the level of meaning, ideologies and cultural values are mediated by public policies and reflected in given types of legislative enactment on industrial democracy.

Unlike economic and technological conditions, the institutional structure of industrial relations shapes some national practices. Again, the processes of institutionalization largely account for the continuation of a characteristic national pattern of industrial democracy and are interlinked with a general evolutionary trend towards greater experimentation encompassing countries in the Second and Third Worlds as well as in the west.

But, if the overall 'shape' of institutional machinery can be substantially accounted for by ideology and other 'subjective' meanings, power explains which forms of industrial democracy predominate. Historically, across the nations, a trend towards a greater degree of institutionalization is apparent, but cyclical movements within this very broad long-run change are no less fundamental. Indeed times of institutional innovation closely parallel the 'waves' of industrial conflict analysed in the previous chapter, typically occurring diverse attempts at accommodation under highly variegated distributions of power.

Strategic choices, rationalities and preferences

In the first place, then, the emergence of given forms of industrial democracy is intimately connected with the overall preferences of the 'actors' themselves.

In the case of employers and managers, the aims of raising profitability, productivity and efficiency are associated with a preference for shop-floor participatory programmes and consultative practices; while the search for harmony and organizational cohesiveness underlies profit sharing. Co-partnership and commonwealth ventures. When labour goals are job regulation and improvements in wages and conditions, trade union and workgroup controls, coupled with collective bargaining, are sought. Finally, for governments and members of the state, a concern to enhance economic and social performance is associated with a preference for facilitative legislation and for the introduction of diverse practices depending on their success.

Strategies and diverse institutional forms

The strategic choices of the 'actors' and their manifold preferences are not always reflected in actual outcomes, not least because the commanding forms in a given country are the product of disparate meanings and constraints and, above all, the distribution of power in the industrial relations system and wider society. But, while there is no universally agreed meaning of industrial democracy its permutations are reflected in at least six main institutional arrangements worldwide: workers' self-management, producer co-operatives, co-determination, works councils and similar institutions, trade union involvement and shop-floor level programmes.

To be sure, while there are notable disparities in institutional practice, *influence* and *involvement* are less varied amongst nations. Thus, as the Industrial Democracy in Europe international Research Group revealed, with the exception of Yugoslavia, a hierarchial pattern of involvement with a typically limited degree of participation by workers is characteristic in Europe. Moreover, with the partial exception of Yugoslavia and Scandinavia, the influence of workers and representative bodies is universally lower than for the highest echelons of management. But for comparative purposes, the thrust of the analysis must concentrate principally on explanations for institutional diversity. And, as is indicated a series of broad cultural values and ideologies, public policies and legislation, the distribution of power in the 'larger' society, aspects of the institutional structure of industrial relations, and power and power conflicts amongst the 'actors' themselves are all relevant here.

Meanings : culture and ideology

Throughout history, Utopian thinkers have argued passionately the feasibility of social and economic organization founded on mutual co-operation for the social good, with he respective talents of all men and women being released and developed to the talents of all men and women being released and developed to the full in an unconstrained and non-exploitative association with their fellows. These ideals have been frequently nurtured by broad cultural values, with commitments such as nurtured by broad cultural values, with commitments such as these being most likely to flourish in countries in which once again: (1) positive views on human nature and 'high trust' relationships prevail; (2) innovation is encouraged; (3) a future orientation facilitates strategic planning involving the workforce; (4) there is an emphasis on 'being' as well as 'doing'; and (5) hierarchical relationships between people are minimized. Taking a number of examples, the industrial democracy framework in West Germany reflects a pronounced "inclination to resolve differences by integrating opposing forces into an institutional organization' by integrating opposing forces into an institutional organization', because 'accommodation and integration, as well as order and authority, occupy an important place in the national system of values'. There has thus been a long history of interest in workers' participation in Germany which persuasively points to a 'culturalist' explanation rather than one rooted in technology or economic conditions, which have altered substantially over the same period of time. Again, the development of the Yugoslavian system of self-management was facilitated by a heterogeneous and decentralized culture, coupled with certain agricultural co-operative practices, including the Balkan phenomenon of zadruga, in which two or three related families jointly owned their means of livelihood and produced and consumed communally. Again, the Mondragon producer co-operatives are closely interconnected with wider cultural and institutional supports and with the strong 'associative spirit' within the basque region as a whole. And, while the IDE researches found that a north-south cultural division within Europe had only a limited impact on levels of influence, it did affect the 'ways in which this influence is achieved. In a sense, too, basic democratic values and practices, by definition, underlie all systems of workers' participation.

Furthermore, no serious analyst of industrial relations would dispute the proposition that the characteristics and objectives of particular types of industrial democracy are infused by general ideologies. The formal arrangements emerging under modern capitalism, managerialism, corporatism, liberal pluralism and social democracy, democratic socialism, state socialism and syndicalism are thus contrasting in institutional structure and conception, if not always in terms of actual effectiveness and practical outcomes. Hence, on the basis of disparate ideological assumptions, radically different varieties of participative machinery have been constructed. The tendency towards 'absolutism' in the French industrial relations system has inhibited reformist moves in the direction of participatory democracy. And, although cultural values have clearly been pervasive in the emergence of participatory institutions in selected eastern European countries moves in this direction have also been justified in ideological terms.

Public policy and legal enactment

But the highest meanings encompassed in cultures and ideologies are also fused at a public policy level and reflected in diverse legal provisions underpinning various institutional arrangements for industrial democracy, the IDE researchers revealing that, in Europe, formal provision for workers' participation is greatest in Yugoslavia, italy, Norway, Sweden, Denmark and West Germany and lowest in Great Britain and Israel. Indeed, four characteristic shapes were discovered: (1) the low-profile pattern, typical of Belgium and Great Britain, in which, with the partial exception of management and representative bodies, all groups have limited participative rights; (2) the hicrarchical one-peaked pattern of France, Norway and Sweden, in which the focus of decision makings the level above top management, (3) the hierarchical two peaked pattern of Denmark, Finland, west Germany, Italy, the Netherlands and Israel and (4) the representative peaked pattern, which is confined to Yugoslavia.

Yet, while it has always been appreciated that the public and legal policies are basic to the different types of institutional machinery until recently it was not fully understood that these also underlie effective participation in terms of influence and involvement. Hence, as the IDE researchers themselves noted:

> high levels of employee participation are a function of an intricate interrelation of internal managerial practices and externally promoted support systems based on formal laws or collective bargaining agreements.
>
> Further, both these variables together do a better job of predicting influence and power distributions than 'objective' technological or structural conditions such as organizational size, internal differentiation, or levels of automation. This last finding underscores the 'voluntaristic' nature of industrial democracy in the sense of being a system which is more the outcome of socio-political factors than of structural opportunities or constraints.

And, above all, 'codification' of participative rights through de jure provisions is an insistent centralized pressure, rooted in public policy and political power, that ensures that a measure of influence passes from top management to the representative channels and which further defines the characteristic institutional shape of given national experiments.

Constraints: structures and institutionalization

However, for the *comparative* analysis of industrial democracy institutions, economic and technological constraints have limited explanatory consequence. Of course, if these forces are analysed historically, then, as Maurice and Sellier have pointed out, the *mode of industrialization* may be 'visible in the system of industrial relations', and certainly in countries such as

Sweden, the concentrated structure of industrial firms may have a bearing upon the institutional structure of collective bargaining and hence upon the patterns of participation. Similarly, in France, the existence of a substantial number of small and medium-sized enterprises could have checked institutional developments in participatory democracy. But, at any given point in time, there are obvious restrictions to this type of explanation because, *in countries with roughly equivalent economic and technical bases, radically divergent patterns of industrial democracy have been established.* For instance, amongst the most successful of the predominantly private enterprise economies, the West German system of co-determination has no obvious parallels in, say, the American or Japanese contexts. Again, in eastern Europe, independent worker's councils have periodically surfaced in Poland and Czechoslovakia (self-management being confined to Yugoslavia) and display few similarities with practices in East Germany or the Soviet Union.

Moreover, at an intermediary analytical level, the role of organizational variables in shaping divergencies in national experiences is circumscribed. Factors such as size and various dimensions of organizational structure as well as the 'cognitive attitudinal' orientations of managers, trade union representatives and workers have very little impact when set against the far greater effects of legal and other institutional supports. Nevertheless, the structure of *industrial relations* institutions does account for some national differences. Collective bargaining at plant level thus tends to be the principal form of industrial democracy when the structure of negotiation is organized at that point but, in its absence, as Clegg has observed, 'there are demands for alternative arrangements to allow workers to exercise some influence over those matters which concern them and which cannot be adequately regulated in industry or regional agreement's. Again, an 'inward shift in the locus of collective bargaining' can have profound repercussions for the characteristics of participatory machinery, which is demonstrated particularly in the transformation of works councils machinery to incorporate trade union representatives. Moreover, in the West German case, legally based works councils and codetermination reflect not only 'the traditional recourse to juridical regulations' but also the centralized structure of collective bargaining, the organization of trade unions on industry lines and the preference of trade unionists for exerting a strategic influence at national level over large-scale social and economic policy, rather than being concerned with the minutiae of plant-level agreements.

On a long-term basis, institutional processes are also vital to the continuation of given practices and are associated with a progressive evolutionary expansion in the machinery of industrial democracy. Hence as the twentieth century has progressed, there has been a predilection for greater institutional innovation in leading western

European countries. The data cover periods when there was either the introduction of a new institutions or an essential extension of the rights of an existing one or the reform of an existing institution and, in addition to facilitative changes, three separate modes of introduction ate identified (informal, collective agreement or statutory law). Fundamentally, too, once the first type of plant-level institution is established, the processes of institutionalization ensure the stability of distinctive machinery and hence a *continued* diversity of pattern amongst nations.

A broad evolutionary trend is also underlined by the institutionalization of industrial democracy in much of eastern Europe, even though, globally, this is likely to *reinforce* disparities in the structure and functions of machinery.

Variety is also currently being encouraged by institutional developments in the Third World with some practices being both is also currently being encouraged by institutional developments in the Third World with some practice being both imaginative sand radical (for instance, in Algeria, provisions in 1971 for the 'socialist management of the enterprise' were contained in Ordinance no. 71-4 and, in the Co-operative Republic Act of 1980 in Guyana, the long-run transformation of both state and private enterprises to workers' co-operatives is envisaged. Above all, workers' congress have proliferated in Chinese enterprises and are designed to buttress self-management in the factory. As it happens, the influence of these bodies has oscillated over time but, by June 1982, they had been instituted in 95 per cent of the big and medium-sized enterprises in China's major industrial cities, their growth being closely linked with policies on decentralization and the move towards a greater degree of "market socialism. The formal powers of the congresses include the discussion, examination and initiation of production targets and plans, the formulation and administration of enterprises policies on labour protection and welfare and a new capacity to elect the factory management. To be sure, their effectiveness depends greatly on the willingness of the Party to reduce its influence on enterprise management and union, and it is certainly arguable that they are no more advanced as forms of industrial democracy than the western European institutions. Nevertheless, for our purposes, what is important to note is the marked acceleration of interest in workplace democratization in Third World countries, reinforcing global variety and indicating an appreciable late-development effect in the attempt to secure the accommodation of interests of the industrial relations parties in the production sphere.

The 'power' of the 'actors'

But if the overall shape of particular institutions for industrial democracy can be largely accredited to distinctive cultural values and ideologies (coupled with the structure of industrial relations institutions) and the extent of formal rules to legislative intervention (linked, in turn, with public policy and state intervention), power is decisive in determining which type emerges as dominant. Hence, although it should be emphasized that major initiatives in workers' participation have almost invariably required a strong presence of workers' associations or a legislature committed to such objectives, substantial divergencies in *practice* are largely based on the distribution of power. A strong presence of the state thus encourages a highly legalistic and regulated mode of participation. When associated with corporatism, the pressure foe social and system integration tends to encourage non-oppositional, consultative modes of participatory machinery at enterprise and workgroup levels. By contrast, in the USA and other countries in which the role of the state has been circumscribed and trade unions are on the decline, many of the most important initiatives have stemmed from human relations-oriented managers. Where trade unions are strong, the development of participative machinery has been typically grounded in collective bargaining and organized on the basis of a single channel of representation. And finally, in cases such as Norway, where the labour movements is powerful, and governmental intervention through social and labour legislation has been marked, experimentation in a range of participative forms has occurred.

Moreover, the distribution of power in the industrial relations system and wider society is basic to the explanation of the *origins* of institutional diversity. But such exigencies have been met with varying responses in particular countries, reflecting not only diverse *strategic choices but, above all, distinctive patterns of power and interaction between the dominant political parties, the state, organized labour and employers.* Moreover so far as institutional processes are concerned, machinery established at an early point in a nation's history constitutes a traditional reference point for solutions to industrial unrest and, even after a period of dormancy, may be reactivated in a similar or modified form at a subsequent period of reconstruction. Indeed, the distribution of power underpins 'cyclical' interpretations of the development of industrial democracy, the historical experience being for the genesis or reform of industrial democracy institutions to occur when labour movements are strong and there has been a crest in a wave of industrial conflict.

In detail, leaving aside the wartime agreements, the upsurge of disputes in the later 1910s and early 1920s was met with various attempts at accommodation. But with the onset of the inter-war depression there was a sharp decline in institutional innovation and, in some cases, employer lock-outs to reverse earlier gains by labour. Moreover, it was only when the depression eased in the later 1930s and when a series of Social Democratic and Popular Front governments emerged to mock the seemingly irresistible advance of Fascism and National Socialism, that the situation began to alter appreciably (the

Scandinavian agreements covering collective bargaining and the Matignon Agreement of 1936 in France are obvious cases in point).

Following the Second World War, the rising influencing of labour in a full employment economy again triggered a number of interesting changes and an appreciable advance in the establishment of machinery for industrial democracy. In some countries this was associated either with the trade unions (the recognition of collective bargaining rights and the growth of shop stewards' systems) or with joint consultation. But other nations experienced major programmes of legislative reform encompassing either co-determination of works councils or both. After the apparently successful institutionalization of industrial conflict between 1950 and the early to mid-1960s, the enthusiasm for institutional reform receded, But this situation altered dramatically following the outbreak of strikes which swept Europe in the late 1960s and early 1970s. In almost every European nation there was thus a major attempt at reinstitutionalization which covered both factory-level recognition of trade union activities and major reforms of company decision-making processes to include codetermination by employee representatives. There were also a number of facilitative milestones, before this era of advance ended in the 1980s with the weakening of labour by economic depression and high unemployment.

Moreover, amongst the countries of western Europe, the degrees of statutory intervention in industrial democracy depends greatly on power relationships in the wider society and particularly on the different reactions by governments in the nineteenth century to the rise of organized labour and to the new employment relationships which emerged when industrialism destroyed the system of medieval guilds. Indeed, Bendix and Rokkan have noted that there were three strategies here; (1) to withhold from workers the freedom of association and the right to combine; (2) to grant the right to form associations but to withhold the right to combine, and (3) to grant both the right to form associations and the right to combine. The state in most countries of continental Europe adopted the first policy, while the second was followed in Ireland and the UK and the third in Scandinavia and Switzerland. Moreover, as sorge has observed, the predominant pattern was for 'a higher degree of repression to be associated with a *higher probability of a legal system of works councils emerging*. Plainly, then, if the right to form associations was denied to trade unions, plant level non-union organs were likely to develop, and conversely, if collective bargaining emerged in the enterprises, additional institutional channels became superfluous. Moreover, when the battle for industrial democracy has to be fought by organized labour against governments as well as against the employers, the upshot was that 'it became likely that the avenue for industrial democracy would be sought with the help of the state's legal machinery, either by the penetration of the state by workers' movements, or by attempts of the state to placate workers by introducing statutory council, or by a mixture of both'.

These historical conditions also underline the vital distinction recently drawn by Teulings between 'corporatist' and 'syndicalist' approaches to industrial democracy in western Europe, the first being highly 'codified' and the second based on worker mobilization through unionization. All these countries have a centralized system of codification, but while three (the Netherlands, Sweden and West Germany) rely almost exclusively on legal procedures, others (Belgium, Italy, the UK and Yugoslavia) have a decentralized system as well. And, above all, these twin strategies of labour reflect deeper temporal patterns of struggle designed to wrest power away from top management, with 'the strength of political pressure, and of trade union activity at the company level', being 'responsible for the present degree of industrial democracy in Europe' and, in important respects. for its principal variations.

The resolution of conflicts of interest in the production sphere through industrial democracy has thus occasioned a rich range of institutional practices worldwide. The origins of this variability have to be sought in the nature of strategic choices informed by wider cultural and ideological meanings, transmitted through public policies and legislative enactments, distinctive institutional practices and given 'constellations' of the distribution of power in the 'larger' society and amongst the 'actors' themselves. Moreover, the limited significance of environmental structures in the overall explanation of the main institutional forms underscores the unequal impact of the main conditions isolated in the overall framework of analysis in each substantive area. In deed, it is an elemental truism, no less applicable to the social science in general than to industrial relations, that the patterning of behaviour is intricate and multi-faceted, requiring sophisticated multi-causal explanations in order to establish the various origins of given phenomena.

3 Research and Theory on Groups in Industry

It is now in order to ask whether the patterns of work behavior and their motivations described in this study are consistent with existing theories and research on work groups in industry. Much research has been done in the field and we should relate the concepts derived from this project to the more inclusive framework provided by other studies.

Much of this chapter, therefore, will be a review of other studies and a comparison of their findings with those described here. An important proportion of these other studies deals with the subject of informal organization and this shall be our focus.

In the preceding chapters, for example, we have used such terms and work group, occupational group and interest group somewhat interchangeably. The concept of the *informal group* has been an important one in the field of industrial relations since the famous Western Electric researchers established their significances as "modifiers" of the behavior visualized by the planners of the formal organization.

The most immediate and meaningful experiences of work for the individual are obtained in the context of his work group and his work associates. He can only experience the large organization by indirection, but membership in the small group contributes directly to the shaping of attitudes and behavior toward the entire world of work. For this reason of potency, therefore, the contribution of the small group to the total organization has been a subject of substantial research by those interested in human relations in industry.

Conceptions of the work group

As Whyte has pointed out, the individual is not a member of a single group within a larger structure. Rather, the individual interacts in a variety of settings within the organization. It is the task of the researcher to identify those interaction patterns which are focused and concentrated so that it is reasonable to speak of a "group." These he distinguishes from patterns which are sufficiently random so that the elaborations of behavior we associate with the internal life of the small group are not present to any significant degree.

If we follow all the members of the organization through their hours on the job, we are likely to be impressed with this very proliferation of memberships. Most apparent even to the untrained eye is membership, except for that unique individual, the president, in a *subordinate group;* that is, the employee shares a common supervisor with a number of colleagues. Distinguishable from this group, but closely related, is a *functional,* or *task group*-those employees who must collaborate in some fashion if the work ask defined by the larger organization is to be accomplished. The boundaries of both of these groups are rather well defined by the larger organization.

However, we see two other kinds of clusterings that tend to overlap and penetrate the organization in unexpected ways. They are not defined by the formal organization and are often included under the general term, informal organization. One of these groups has received a great deal of attention from researchers, the *friendship clique,* whose members are attracted to each other because they gain certain satisfactions from their interactions as such. The other type of group tha is less well studied but, we feel, equally important, is the *interest group*. It is comprised of employees who share a common economic interest and who are held together by their desire to gain common objectives within the larger organization.

The memberships in these groups are not exclusive; there are many overlappings. Our problem here is to gain some perspective on their interrelations. To do this we shall take a rather close look at some approaches to the study of both the friendship groups or cliques and the task group. From that vantage point we should be able to identify the distinctive characteristics of our interest groups.

The friendship clique

This might well be conceived as the elementary building block of human organization. As Mayo writes, "Man's desire to be continuously associated with his fellows is a strong, if not the strongest human characteristic.

At the workplace we thus find an intricate maze of friendship groups representing the diverse interests of the workers who have been placed there by the organization. The exact boundaries of these multiple clusterings appear to reflect the off-the-job interests and associations of the employees, or their previous work experience. As common observation would have it, like-minded individuals are attracted to one another. Age, ethnic background, outside activities, sex, material status, and so on, comprise the mortar that binds the clique together.

Zeleznik, for example, in his study of a department of relatively unskilled female manual workers, describes this labyrinth of social organization:

There were mainly female operators on the line, who varied from girls in their late teens to middle-aged women with grown families. Age, and hence common interests, seemed to be one of the dividing lines that marked the organization of informal groups within the line. The older women seemed to group together, while a number of the very young girls who were about to be married or who were contemplating marriage, tended to keep together. Operators #1 and #2 were young men in their late teens or early twenties, and they generally kept apart from the girls on the line. A number of women on the line were divorcees and some of them formed their own little group. Still another social grouping was formed by a few women in their early thirties who had been floaters, or utility operators, in th old plant; these operators were faster workers than the average girl on the line, and they knew more of the work positions on the line as a direct result of their having been floaters in the old plant. Although there seemed to be a clustering of girls in one social group or another, as expressed by their choice of company during the rest periods, the groups tended also to shift somewhat; and a girl could, in some cases, be numbered in, or on the fringe of, several of the informal groups.

From the point of view of the administrator, of what significance are these groups?

An assumption often made concerning these social groups is their universality. Arensberg, in reviewing the Mayo research studies, draws the clearest picture of the indispensable function being served:

There was at hand the notion that the function of social relationships is to bolster the individual, to let him healthily act out his feelings, rather than, sickly, to bottle them up or invert them, to give him motivation, identification and willingness to accept the tight new rationalist controls over work, imposed by taskmasters, now taking the place of older but now dead customary controls. Out of Mayo's watching these worker-to-worker relationships of a new sort unite the lonely, embittered apathetic workers of the mule-spinning room, the doctrine of "informal organization" or "teamwork" seems to have been born.

The friendship group has emerged as the agency which welds the individual to the organization. Loyalty, even attachment, to the total organization with its impersonality, extended hierarchy, and social distance becomes ambiguous. However, attachment to the immediate and easily perceived face-to-face group is the predominant reality of organization experience. For the individual it provides a source of personal security in an impersonal environment. As a result, we are not surprised at the striking results obtained in the study of the American soldier, indicating the importance of the primary group in motivation.

Where cliques are largely nonexistent, as they were in the tumultuous aircraft plants of California which expanded literally overnight into huge aggregations of employees, turnover can be enormous. The presumption is that stable social groups take time to crystallize: during the period of formation many potential members will leave voluntarily because they do not find an established unit with which they can affiliate.

Lombard and Mayo conclude that the naive administrator who seeks to break up these cliques because of the inefficiency and wasted motion of the purely social activities involved, is actually doing a dis-service to the organization. In fact, they find that it takes skillful leadership to encourage their formation, at least in organizations undergoing rapid expansion.

Serious criticism of the universal efficacy of friendship cliques involves consideration of personality differences and work structure differences. A well-known study of "rate busters" and output re-stricters disclosed a significant minority who were indifferent, if not hostile, to the social groupings they found on the job.

A recent examination of British longshoremen finds that approximately half of the longshoremen on the docks studied have purposely avoided the social entanglements of work group membership. Given an opportunity to join semi permanent gangs, they prefer random work assignments that leave them free to come and go at will, with no responsibility. In terms of their personalities, this way is more satisfying to them.

The formation of social groups also appears to be a function of the structure of the work situation itself. Argyris, in a recent study of human relations in a New England bank, finds that the incidence of informal social groupings among tellers is less than for bank employees who do not have that high degree of interaction with customers.

Efforts to find universal solutions to the problems of productivity within the dynamics of the friendship group have not been successful.

Some of the earliest research on productivity was based on the assumption that internal harmony in a work group-reciprocated positive feelings-would produce desirable job performance. Increasingly, however, researchers have become disillusioned with the relationship between social satisfaction and worker effort. Perhaps one of the most telling blows to the impetus to devote substantial energies to building work groups that are socio metrically sound is the provocative study by Goods and Fowler in a low morale plant. They found the informal relationships which developed were such as to maintain pressures toward high production in the face of considerable animosity toward the owners and among the workers themselves. Although their findings are severely limited by a unique industrial environment, it has been recognized that the relation between friendship and output cannot be expressed by a simple function.

More recently, Seashore finds in an interesting study in a large heavy equipment manufacturing company that highly cohesive work groups are more likely to have output records that diverge in either direction from plant averages. Tightly knot work groups are almost as likely to have notably poor production records as they are likely to have outstandingly good production records. Several years ago a research report on productivity among clerical workers presented what were generally similar findings:

......it was found that there were great differences in the level of production from one friendship group to another...the friendship groups had their own groups standards; some to work hard and some to take it easy; some to identify with management and others to aggress against management.

A recent well-received text in the field of public administration comes out strongly on the side of encouraging on-the-job social life to facilitate productivity:

Although there is some contradictory evidence, the preponderance of evidence indicates that production is actually increased when social conversation is allowed.... Restrictions that have the effect of diminishing the pleasantness of the work situation rob th workers of a significant source of satisfaction and can be expected, therefore, to reduce their efforts.

However, a study employing methods of precise interaction observation is unique in casting some doubts as to the positive correlation between social interaction and productivity.

The factory department under discussion seems to show that there is a limit to the supposed relation between an increase in "informal social relations" and an increase in productivity.

Thus the administrator is left with some degree of uncertainty as to the significance of these groupings to his organization.

The task group

In recent years the emphasis in human relations

research on work groups has sifted towards greater consideration of the organization of work itself. The layout of the plant and the flow of work provided by the industrial engineer and the placement of supervision controlled by the organizational chart serve to build informal group structures as much as the discovery of common interests and the need for social interaction.

In turn these groups develop norms of behavior and attitude which affect significantly worker effort and loyalty. Most of these center around the interest of the group in controlling: (a) the work methods, (b) output standards or productivity, and (c) relative compensation and prestige relationships. Let us examine each of these in turn.

(a) *Impact on work methods*. The analogy might be to an electrical current which seeks the path of least resistance. The experience of working in close proximity on a day-to-day basis induce methods that may depart from the organization's original conception of the job, or at least it fills in the specified in the formal work plan. For example, on repetitive jobs employees find it more pleasant to exchange jobs, although such trading is illegal. In the automobile industry, it is a common phenomenon for one worker to do two jobs, while a colleague enjoys and extended rest. Employees changes the sequence in which operations are to be performed in order to reduce job tensions and provide short cuts.

Some of these informal, or should we say

unplanned for, work methods may decrease worker output. Workers' machinations can overstate make-ready time during job changes. However, other worker innovation undoubtedly increase the total product. One of the most striking cases of the latter was observed by Gross. He found that radar teams through communications circuits set up during social periods off-the-job were compensating for deficiencies in the information provided by the formal organization. the additional networks provided spontaneously contributed significantly to job success. These informal groups provided interactions which can improve team coordination vastly.

Similarly, researchers have analyzed the initiative exhibited by a group of department store salesmen in evolving a new work pattern that solved a serious internal morale problem, which had been created by a new incentive system. The innovation was so successful both in eliminating interpersonal frictions and in fostering high productivity that top management eventually encouraged its spread to other units of the organization. As the authors conclude: ".... under further specified conditions the work unit may make and execute decisions ordinarily considered managerial.

Aside from evolving methods which seem most convenient to work group members, the pattern of doing the job is fitted to the status system of the group. Members with most prestige, if at all possible, receive the best jobs. Where possible, working location and equipment are similarly assigned. And where these are not under group control, helping and trading can be adjusted to the status system. The exchange-of-favors system readily responds to the prestige hierarchy. Of course, the evaluation placed on jobs-the differentiation of the more preferred from the less preferred - is itself a product of group interaction.

Whether due to apparent convenience or the exigencies of the status system, the methods evolved within the group for task completion become firmly established. Where outside forces threaten to induce changes, the ranks close and resistance is applied. In part, of course, this may be the natural reaction of the culprit fearing punishment for rule infractions. A more reasonable explanation of the informal group's resistance to change, however, is the intimate relationship between the task group as an entity and the work methods they have evolved. A threat to one is a real threat to the other.

(b) *Impact on Output Standards.* Probably more attention has been given to this aspect of task group behavior than to any other. Starting with the work of Mathewson, and extending through the Western Electric studies, we have a long and distinguished line of studies indicating that work groups often formulate quite specific output standards and obtain close conformity from their members in maintaining these standards. Productivity itself is increasingly conceived as a group phenomenon.

There have been several reasons advanced why output control occupies a place of such importance in the life of the group. Work standards are one of the most important aspects of the job which can in some fashion be influenced by worker action. The difficulty of the job, the energy expenditure it requires, is largely determined by the number of units required, rather than by the nature of the job itself. Presumably, without group control management would be able to utilize individual differences and competition for promotion and greater earnings, to establish higher and higher output or performance standards. This would penalize particularly the slower worker and the older employee. It might, however, penalize all workers by cutting piece rates where they exist and reducing the number of employees required by the operation. "Run away" output may have internal ramifications. We have observed situations where group controls were weak, and younger, low-prestige employees exceeded the production and earnings records of their betters. The results were calamitous for the internal status hierarchy of the department and ultimately for the effectiveness of the formal organization.

Thus output control is a basic objective of group action as well as an essential element i maintaining group stability. Not only the relation of the members to one another, but the durability of the worker's relation to hs job depends on the efficiency of this process. Again we need to note that the resultant is not always unfavorable to management. We have many instances on record where the work group has sanctioned increasingly high productivity.

It should be evident that a great deal of the interest in informal group relations is the product of this presumed relation between output standards evolving within the group and actual worker productivity. There have been many efforts to find the magic formula that would convert low group norms to high group norms.

The evolution of the method of *group decision* for gaining acceptance for changes in production methods and output standards is recognition of the potency of group standards. The theory presumes that leadership methods that involve the entire work group in the change process have two major advantages:

(1) They can eliminate the major barrier of existing group standards which militate against any change, per se.

(2) More positively, they commit the individual to new efforts in the context of his group membership. In a sense, the individual "promises" his fellows to accomplish some change in his behavior. Valuing the opinions of his associates, he feels bound to maintain his agreement.

Ideally, the decision itself becomes the new standard or norm of conduct for the task group. Also, efforts to develop plant-wide incentive systems are premised on the assumption that output and effort are dependent on the relations of the work group to the total social system of the plant.

We find that quality also has a group standard. There are many instances when the management seeks to *reduce* quality, but the work-manship norm resists such changes. This situation is particularly true in skilled groups where management may feel that undue effort is being applied to maintain standards and tolerances that are unnecessary in the light of the eventual use of the product.

(c) *Impact on Relative Compensation and Prestige Relations*. The fact that jobs take on a significant social meaning can be seen in the importance attached to wage differentials within the group itself. For example, we have many instances on record where management assigned an equal value to each job and the group found significant distinguishing characteristics. Certain jobs are ranked by employees as *more important or desirable,* and these are expected to have higher earnings than lower ranked jobs. At times, management's own evaluation process will contribute directly to these rankings. The established hierarchy is reinforced, of course, over time, by th gradual perfection of the correlation between the esteem accorded particular workers and the prestige accorded to their jobs. The "more important" workers have moved to the "more important" jobs. Problems occur only when changes are introduced which violate the established hierarchy.

Some common features of these groups

Although these several concepts of the informal group are not identical, and in some cases not even complementary in their basic dimensions, they do have one common feature. All emphasize equilibrium: the development of a system of interpersonal relations which stabilizes the work situation an interconnected series of friendship linkages, work-flow relations, output levels, and status-income relations. The objectives are the maintenance of individual and group stability by insuring a predictability of day-to-day events and effecting a modus vivendi between individual on-the-job needs and the requirements of the formal organization.

The clusterings of workers-on-the-job all have these characteristics.

The sum of a group of individuals is something more than the total of the constituents, it is a new organization. Because most of the members obtain satisfaction in gaining acceptance as a part of the group, and the group itself wields an influence over its members, there are pressures toward conformity within the group. These pressures result in th establishment of accepted ways of living together. The way of life includes a complex system of customs and rules, vested interests, and interaction patterns which govern the relationship of members of the group to one another and to the larger environment of which it is a part.

The informal group in any and all of its

meanings serves well-recognized and accepted human needs. Its existence and continued preservation are hardly matters for surprise. The building up of routines, of established methods of accomplishing tasks, of predictable social relationships, of groups roles-these are all elements of structuring which social scientists have found to be typical of the human group. They define the group.

Particularly, through the setting and maintenance of group standards, informal groups have protected their memberships from possible indiscretions that might reflect adversely on them all; also they have provided support for the individual, by acting as a buffer to outside organizations, and by sustaining him through the provision of known and acceptable routines of behaving within the face-to-face work group.

Thus the informal group, as perceived in such studies, reacts to the initiations of other organizations, particularly management. Defined in equilibrium terms, the reaction is always an attempt to preserve or regain the previous undisturbed state-to protect the work methods, social relations, and output levels incorporated in the norms of the group. The goal is always one of security, maintaining the status quo, although, as Humans points out above, the whole protective process is best conceived, not as "deliberate planning" but as an "automatic response" to the industrial system.

Although it has been possible to explain a

great deal of in-plant worker behavior in terms of the elaborations induced by informal, ace-to-face groups, an element has been lacking. As a result, research studies demonstrate inconsistent or inconclusive findings. The problem appears to center around the concept of the informal group as something apart from the dynamic, collective bargaining environment, and as dependent on immediate, highly personal intragroupe relations.

Mutual economic interest as the group focus

We have been describing in all of the previous chapters how the organization of the plant provides incentives for the banding together of individual workers into interest groups. These incentives are not only the desire to protect the status quo, work standards, degree of rule enforcement and discipline meted out by supervision, relative earnings, and seniority position, but also include the opportunity to improve their relative position. Improvements can take the form of looser standards, a preferred seniority position, more overtime, more sympathetic supervision, correction of inequities, and better equipment. Many of these benefits often substitute for the more traditional kinds of promotions and mobility.

Although the dictums of personnel administration could lead us to believe that relative wage rates, incentive earnings, promotional ladders, layoff schedules, overtime distribution, quality of working conditions, and work loads are distributed among work groups on the basis of a comprehensive program or system that is independent of pressures, this ideal is rarely attained in practice, if indeed it is an ideal. Work groups do compete among themselves for the available economic rewards.

The distribution of these benefits may be much influenced by the pressures of united and determined informal groups. What management feels is "equitable," just as what the union determines is in the "members' interest," is determined to a large extent by the attitudes expressed by those individuals who can support their demands by group reinforcements. The reality of the in-plant situation offers organized workers many benefits and penalizes relatively, and on occasion absolutely, those work groups which for one reason or another are unable to exercise similar power in the market place of the plant.

At the outset many of these groups may have defensive motives. As Barkin notes in reviewing the organizing history of unions themselves:

> The early efforts of job groups tend to be defensive. They try to keep conditions from getting worse, to protect members of the groups and to prevent destruction of the group itself.

However, it becomes apparent that it is impossible to stand still. maintaining the same conditions, in a dynamic plant, means sustaining a relative decline in benefits in comparison with those attained by other groups. As in the broader political environment, eternal vigilance is the price of equitable treatment. Even if others were not fighting for increased shares of the economic pie, management is making so many changes in equipment, scheduling, supervision, work methods, and all the rest, that a static position is out of th question.

To repeat, this is not th traditional concept of the informal group seeking conformity with established norms of conduct. These are much more free enterprise units, interacting in a struggle for maximization of utility. This is not to imply that all such groups are equally aggressive in the struggle for self-improvement, or equally wall equipped with all the wherewithal to do battle via the union and management grievance procedure and more direct pressure tactics. Some lack the spirit of combat, others the means, whereas only a restricted few are endowed with the characteristics associated with sustained activity and progress toward the goals they seek.

Much of what we say implies a degree of dual or even treble disloyalty. Other groups-management, the union, and fellow workers -are perceived as either barriers to or sources of assistance to be manipulate at will.

We were often surprised at the absence of loyalties across group boundaries. Workers showed very little sympathy for the problems of fellow employees and would even injure the standing of other employees to improve their own conditions.

For example, in the cushion department of a large automobile body plant, the so-called "pad-up operation comes before the actual upholstering of the automobile seat. The latter group, called cushion builders, have been traditionally higher skilled and paid, although the wage differential is no longer significant. Nevertheless, they feel themselves very superior to the pad-up men. Management, however, estimates that it takes substantially longer to break in a pad-up man, and his job content requires greater effort. Recently, when models changed and job content was being reapportioned, the cushion builders used their economic strength to shift still additional duties to the pad-up men for which they will not b compensated and which must be performed within the same time period.

From the point of view of the interest group, it is not high identification or loyalty that counts, but rather the right tactics in using or ignoring these other aggregations. Thus, management is neither good nor bad, liked nor disliked as such. In fact, this approach suggests that it may not always be fruitful to think in promanagement and prounion terms. It may well be, as we have suggested, that a group which is satisfied with itself, with its ability to protect and improve its own interests, is more favorable to both union and management.

Although the adoption of the club form and a formal name for their group was unique, the association of men sharing common work-created needs is not unusual. In every plant thee will be countless numbers of such groups ranging from a short-lived protest movement that attempts to secure higher rates for several men assigned to a newly installed conveyer in a shipping department, to an institutionalized group like the sprayers, who have long-run, continuing problems of mutual concern. Some of these groups begin to hold meetings, either under the aegis of the union, or in spite of it. Some begin to look upon a particular steward as their representative and struggle to elect a man who will defend their interests. A few even adopt written constitutions that define their objectives and their methods of attainment.

Their membership is not limited necessarily to the small face-to-face group. Unlike some of th social groupings described above, their size is not limited by the ability of the individual to respond to others in day-to-day interactions. Whereas so-called primary groups rarely exceed a dozen workmen, inserted interest bodies may contain a hundred or more workers sharing common objectives and acting in concert to further them.

The results for the larger plant may not be a system tending toward equilibrium at all. One the basis of this study we might expect that certain combinations of pressure groups actually involve the organization in increasing instability-a trend toward disequiliburium. We have observed plants where the interaction of these groups involves increasingly greater discontent, turmoil, and non-adaptive behavior; that is, their behavior tends to reinforce the very problems it was designed to solve.

Similarly, the internal structure of these groups is much more responsive to changes in their external environment than is often implied in the concept of the informal work group as a relatively durable, impervious entity. Overnight, technical changes introduced by management can convert a cohesive task force into a disunited rabble, squabbling over internal differences. Similarly, we have observed group of weakly united employees become a force of some magnitude in the social system of the plant within a brief period, with no changes in personnel.

Most important, these interest interest groups are not static self-preservation societies. Rather they are engaged in the active pursuit of the economic welfare of their membership. Not all of their behavior is intelligently contrived to win the goals they seek, nor are th goals always well-designed or understood, but their basic orientation never changes. Like the union, they want more and more-and still more. The specific goals themselves are not constant, but are continually in flux, as the seniority of th workers in the unit changes as other groups attain or fail to attain certain concessions from management, as the union bargaining platform changes, and as management introduces new equipment and new personnel. In the process these groups contribute much to shaping the industrial relations climate of the plant.

There is no implication that this study has discovered the interest group. On the contrary, many others have preceded us. Two studies are particularly worthy of mention:

In a less well-known section of the now famous Yankee City series the authors make what was at that time a startling observation. In the pre-World War II Newburyport shoe factories, workers' earning did not correlate very well with the respective skill levels. The authors give a specific example in comparing the earnings of the men in th wood heel departments with those of the makers. Making is a relatively skilled occupation in the shoe factory, compared to the heel department; yet the earnings were substantially higher in the wood heel department. As the authors conclude, "The special explanation for this fact lay in the solidarity of the workers in this department."

4 Managerial Strategies and Industrial Relations

So far out principal aim has been to identify managers as a special occupational group and to outline not only patterns of recruitment into positions within the administrative hierarchy and the basic components of managerial activities themselves but also the saliency, in the industrial relations context, of concepts such as corporate control and professional aspiration which constitute nominalist definitions of modern managerial personnel. At this juncture, therefore, it is clearly apposite for a shift in the focus of out review to accommodate a broad ranging inspection of the industrial relations policies of managers in disparate national and enterprise situations. Nevertheless, although the fundamental role of strategy insofar as workplace attitudes and behaviour are concerned has been acknowledge in the literature, hitherto the bulk of the accounts have tended to constitute articles of faith bereft of rigorous empirical support or anchorage in deductive analytical precept; the qualities which, together, constitute the elemental foundations of a genuine social science.

In this chapter, then, two major concerns will be uppermost. First, within the province of industrial relations, it will be our endeavour to chart the foremost influences upon the genesis of identifiable managerial strategies. And second, we shall seek to deploy propositions derived from a general conceptual model as a base for clarifying subsequent analyses. These, in their turn, embrace: (a) social responsibility within the modern business enterprise and in its relationships with the environment; (b) policies on payment systems and remuneration and (c) control and industrial democracy.

A word is in order at the outset, however, concerning out overall treatment of the notion of managerial strategy itself. Indeed, it is worth emphasising that, in our basic interpretation, we have sought to articulate the respective concepts of 'choice' and 'constraint' which to date, have constituted focal points in the opposing schools ongoing disputation. That is to say, while it is undoubtedly out view that a series of so-called 'structural' 'subjective' and 'power' in strategy in concrete social formations; equally, a considerable measure of divergence is still a manifest consequence of strategic choices being exercised between a range of possible types of action, which, while being informed by orientations and perceptions, remain tributes to the independent creative power of social actors in given industrial relations systems.

In general vein, therefore, as may be seen from the accompanying figure, the principal components of the model incorporate four fundamental analytical categories: (1) at the highest level of abstraction, structural and environmental constraints coupled with dominant modes of rationality and the role of cultural variables (2) at an intermediary level, managerial organizational structures within the enterprise itself alongside the institutional structure of industrial relations; (3) the orientations and perceptions of the principal actors; (4) the power of the major industrial relations parties and interest groups. These points of analytical differentiation, too, provide useful foundations for out extrapolation, in the ensuring discourse, of the thesis of the relationship between constraints and choice in the germination of industrial relations strategies themselves.

Structural constraints, rationality and culture

To begin with, therefore, managerial strategies may be understood as being occasioned by a constellation of political and economic forces, which, in the main, set boundaries to the probable strategic choice which eventuate in given social structures. Naturally, the implementation of strategies will in themselves depend greatly upon a series of further conditioning variables such as managerial organization, patterns of authority within the management hierarchy, and, above all, upon the power of oppositional groups. But equally politico-economic movements and structures in the wider enterprise environment are crucial in two main respects: first, they place certain identifiable limitations upon the total amount of control vested in members of the enterprise; and second, they will tend to direct choices along particular channels while curtailing other modes of initiative.

More formally, then, strategies of managerial personnel in industrial relations may be expected to vary substantially in the following politico-economic situations:

1. Predominately private enterprise
   (a) Large-scale joint stock companies
   (i) limited state involvement
   (ii) 'dirigiste' or corporatist planning
   (b) Small-scale private companies
   (c) Public sector enterprises
   (i) Centralised
   (ii)Decentralised
2. State-socialist and market socialist enterprises
   (a) Directive planning
   (b) Guided market system
   (c) Decentralised market economy

It is clear, therefore, that the control exercised by mangers over commercial and technical as well as personnel questions in the enterprise itself may be subject to widespread variation in given politico-economic contexts, not only because of, say, the differences in power of indigenous labour movements but also according to the amount of control at the discretion of managerial and non-managerial employees vis-a-vis state planning agencies, owners, of capital, shareholders and so on respectively. And, above all, the 'decomposition' of state or owner control or the expanding influence of the enterprise over the environment or, again, the degree of decentralisation of the economy and polity all undoubtedly enhance the range and scope of issues actually *managed* in the enterprise itself. By the same token, if the organization in question becomes a receding locus of power, the cession of widespread employee 'rights', the growth of decisive managerial strategies on payment systems and principles of remuneration, and the emergence of comprehensive industrial democracy institutions, may amount to little more than empty pieties having virtually no impact upon actual behaviour in the concerns in question whatsoever.

But although the above classification of politico-economic environments accommodates a wide range of types, insofar examples deserve special emphasis: (a) the effects of market conditions; (b) the consequences of corporatist planning; and (c) state involvement in public sector establishments and in predominately public enterprise economies respectively.

Market constraints upon managerial strategies

It has been a commonplace, of course, in Marxist writings on industrial relations to emphasis that managerial strategies are typically patterned by market conditions under the control of capital.

Indeed, a familiar assumption here has been that the logic of the free enterprise system ultimately imposes fundamental limitations on managerial action ruling out, say, 'humanist' or welfare-oriented policies at least in the long-term. Human has thus stressed such a view: "The development of industrial relations has been powerfully influenced by the structure and dynamics of capitalism and by the strategies of employers. The determining impact of capital has been reinforced by the largely capitalism is reflected in industrial relations. The goals of further investment and stable prices point naturally to the need for a shift in the balance of power between capital and labour, between profits and salaries. The necessary strategy for employers involves restraint on workers' incomes, an intensification of work pressure and labour discipline, a reinforcement of managerial control at the point of production."

Yet rigorous empirical demonstrations of such a thesis have not been conspicuous landmarks of the industrial relations literature. Indeed, probably the most sophisticated attempt to trace the relationship between market exigency and managerial strategy appeared a quarter of a century ago, in Gouldner's classic, *Wildcat Strike*. After all, Goldener, it will be recalled, deployed the epithet 'willing but unable' to designate the conduct of mangers in the events preceding what must be the most familiar documentation of a strike in the voluminous sociological and industrial relations writings on this theme. Moreover, the 'need' of managers to define their 'status prerogatives' was also traced to 'the market economy in which it operate'; since, in 'a market economy, the status and legitimate expectations of the parties involved, are registered in the contract and in the interpretations placed upon it; over time these establish a cumulative body of precedent.

By the same token, in Gouldner's view, whenever serious industrial relations problems were encountered, the tendency for managerial personnel to experience an acute sense of indecisiveness was also directly attributed to the market. For, precisely because in a fully operating market economy the decisions vested in *managerial* personnel tend to be circumscribed by external pressures, action at enterprise level may, in turn, be constrained in four major respects: (1) the undue caution which may cripple initiative where decisive decision is really required; (2) the cost calculability which is almost invariably assigned to workers' claims (even on questions of a non-pecuniary character); (3) the tendency to orient decisions to those of competitors; and (4) the unpredictability and changeability of the wider environment which undermines the workability of specific Industrial relations contracts and induces an excessive caution in the formulation of advanced labour policies themselves.

The trend towards corporatism

Yet from a variety of normative standpoints the gradual erosion of market mechanisms and their replacement by state planning agencies has been identified as a dominant trend amongst the various economic and industrial changes of the twentieth century. This recognition has been evident above all, of course, in the debates in and around corporatist systems, which, despite the variations in conception, share the common disavowal of fundamental class conflicts in modern social formations and the focus instead upon the mechanisms for creating functional interests based on the division of labour in societies bonded by organic solidarity. To be sure there remains a crucial distinction here between state and societal corporatism; for, while in the first case, interest representation is imposed and authoritarian leaving comparatively little freedom for manoeuvre for managerial personnel, in the second, the gradual replacement of liberal democratic systems has been viewed as largely spontaneous process with the rights and influence of organizations being demanded of rather than enforced by the state itself. Again, on the basis of the assumptions of the latter thesis, the impetus for corporatism may, in turn, be consequential, at least in part, upon employers' and managers' associations seeking the assistance of the state for investment capital, the protection of markets from external competition, the underwriting of advanced technologies which might otherwise be precluded by cost or risk and not least, of course, as a means for containing the industrial relations consequences of the growth in the influence and power of labour movements.

Indeed, there are now several detailed reviews of the likely consequences of any trend towards corporatism for industrial relations strategies of managers. But from an analytical standpoint, Winkler's classification provides the best general framework. For him, then, the corporatist commitment to unity and order in employment relations would tend to produce the following policies within the enterprise.

Ideological Slogn	Operating Principles	Specific Policies
Unity	Co-operation	Price control. Industrial Reorganization. State organized cartels.
Order	Discipline	Wage-salary control. Prohibition of strikes and
lockouts.	Compulsory	Arbitration. Inquisitional Tribunals.

From an analytical standpoint, however, the direct effects of state involvement upon managerial strategy within the private sector have seldom been fully explored although Claus Offe's *Industry and inequality* provides valuable insights into the probable erosion of 'the achievement principle' and its replacement by radically divergent modes of enterprise authority and types of reward system consequent upon such an exigency. Offe's basic distinction thus focused upon the contrast between so-called 'task-continuous status organizations' and 'task- discontinuous status organizations' in the former type 'to be higher in the organization's status hierarchy is to have more of the same skills than someone in a lower position', while, in the latter, 'someone in the lower position has *different* skills'. But with the increasing dependency of the organization on the state, the second type tends to predominate and hence, instead of rewards being based upon the technical criteria of competence and performance, new mechanisms of control appear in which 'peripheral' elements of the work role- the normative and ideological requirements- become increasingly salient. In short, the effect of state involvement is to direct managerial strategies for reward and remuneration away from achievement and towards ascriptive criteria and, in essence, from technical and economic to power and political consideration which ultimately inform policy in any fully-fledged corporatist society.

State involvement in the socialist economy

Managerial strategies in industrial relations may also be affected, however, by state intervention in socialist-type economic systems. Hence, in a system of so-called directive planning, as Crompton and Gubbay have observed:- "the overall plan is devised by central agencies for approval and modification by the highest political authorities....Plans will cover the whole scope of economic activity-manpower requirements and availability, investment in each industry, physical inputs and outputs from industry, credit, taxation, prices, wages, total consumption, the composition of state expenditure and so on. Central plans are refined by successive specialist agencies on a sectoral and territorial basis, where the task of such lower-level be realised. Eventually each enterprise will be set a battery of goals such as minimal targets for physical output, labour productivity and accounting profits." By contrast, however, in guided market systems, elements of which may be detected in selected Eastern European countries, considerable scope for decision making is devolved to enterprises and, in such a milieu, "enterprise managers have an area of freedom". Again, most significantly of all, in market socialist systems a measure of autonomy and a facility to generate fully-fledged strategies in labour and industrial relations may well be evident. Certainly, as well shall see in the section on industrial democracy, even if cost conscious considerations become gradually more ascendant, at the same time, *pari passu*, a market socialist system, far from constraining managerial freedom of action on personnel and industrial relations policy, has considerably enhanced its scope of operation at the expense of planning agencies of the state.

General types of rationality and cultural variables

Notwithstanding the manifest constraints upon managerial strategy occasioned by forces of a structural character, to view these as determinants of industrial relations programmes is still, in out view, a highly unsatisfactory procedure: indeed, such a position reflects both theoretical and substantive shortcomings. After all, not of rationality, in which almost be definition, all industrial relations *strategies* are ultimately grounded, but also, it leads the analyst to ignore almost entirely the distinctive cultural traditions which are manifestly infused in managerial practices. Moreover, as a consequence of the prescriptive notions incorporated in the analytical categories, the crucial role of social choice in the formulation of strategy tends to be 'organized out' of the explanatory framework completely. Yet the very conception of strategy incorporates at root the idea of an overall design within social action and a considerable measure of rationality and calculus in the arrangement of constituent elements themselves.

In the context of industrial relations, then, three man types of rationality would appear to be cardinal: purposive, value and system. Hence, as Mueller has insisted the original Weberian notions may be expanded and refined to encapsulate the following "mutually irreducible substantive types of rationality; (1) Zweckrationalitaet which is social and conative in character; (2) Wertrationalitaet which is subjective and idealistic in character, and (3) Systemrationalitaet which is objective and technical in character"

The domain of purposive rationality thus encompasses 'the realm of material interests' and their articulation in the goals of 'achievement, efficiency and competitions. Moreover, to these familiar concerns of managerial personnel may be added that for status and a 'will to power' reflected in the attempt to control the elemental principles of any emerging industrial relations policy itself. By contrast, value-rational action "is oriented towards moral, disinterested idealistic goals". Again, in more general and identification and elicit' rationalisations' in the sense of Freud and 'legitimation' and 'ideology' in the sense of Weber, Mannbeim and Marx". Finally systemic rationality is "objective, technical and formal". It is in particular associated with technocratic modes of action and is, "in consequence, the formal technical *Systemationalitaet* "commends technology and science but not social interaction". But equally, at the general level, structural exigencies and these general domains of rationality are ultimately transmitted within concrete social formations through dominant cultural traditions. Indeed, as we shall observe in the following section, not only does the concept managerial strategy in different national contexts, in which, identified; serves as a bridge between classical industrial relations and sociological theory in this particular sphere.

"Organizational structures, institutions and managerial strategy

Turning at this point, therefore, to examine a series of middle range analytical constructs and the saliency of these for understanding the emergence of managerial strategies in industrial relations two major approaches will be identified: first, the literature in which organizational variables have been regarded as crucial; and second, those institutional-type propositions which have featured prominently in the corpus of industrial relations scholarship itself.

Organizational variables and management strategy in industrial relations

It has long been understood that industrial relations experiences ay vary greatly between different firms and establishments in the same country as well as across national frontiers. Moreover, it has also be recognised that these differences provision for industrial relations". For although as we have seen the propensity for the formulation of strategies may be constrained by broad politico-economic and cultural variables; equally, organizational characteristics may well, in turn, affect the particular types which become dominant and their ultimate influence on the conduct of industrial relations.

But again, in researches undertaken so far, the studies in which the association between organizational structure, managerial strategy and industrial relations has been systematically analyzed are by no means extensive. To be sure, the germs of such a theory appeared in Woodward's demonstration of the effects of technology upon managerial organization in which certain residual consequences of the main propositions were sketched for the industrial relations situation. But the study by Turner, Roberts and Roberts remains the most fluent account and, indeed, as these authors set out to show, structures of managerial organization would clearly seem to affect propensity to strike in the enterprise itself. After all, strike incidence would appear to be positively correlated with 'standardisation' and 'formalisation' in general management and especially with 'formalisation in industrial relations' and 'facilities for shop stewards'. Again, firms with a high strike proneness were 'essentially bureaucratic in their organization, and therefore inflexible by comparison with those in the 'medium' category. There, high centralisation of decision-making went with a relative absence of customary practice or formal regulation'.

By the same token, although to some extent their evidence was of an illustrative rather than verificatory nature, for Turner and his colleagues it was clear that 'managerial personality' affected industrial relations. Hence, the authors contrasted what they regarded as the predominant British style of management with more rapacious American practices. Yet even in the former case a considerable degree of choice was still manifest since, certain British managerial personnel has also developed strong *Wertrational* strategies for dealing with the workforce and has therefore developed qualities of 'paternalism' or 'ambitions to maintain a high moral tone'.

Institutional approaches

At a high level of abstraction, as we have seen, 'purpose', 'value' and 'system' rationality may be identified as providing general premises which inform managerial strategies in industrial relations. Yet, particularly insofar as international comparisons of industrial relations systems are concerned, a focus upon the consequence of culture has proved to be particularly fruitful as a basis for general explanation. Indeed, industrial relations scholars have typically identified a range of institutional forms which ensure some patterning of social action in specific enterprises and which constitute, in turn, of situations. Of course, the early institutionalist accounts were predominantly descriptive in character, but, as Sorage has pointed out in the context of the genesis of institutions are typically made". Moreover, "from the constellations of constraints to rationality of solutions to the problem of system integration... it will be possible to predict not only the shape the new institutions take, but also the social values that become attached to the practice of industrial relations, i.e. the ideologically emergent goals". Hence, by focusing given historical epochs, it is possible to marry conventional types of institutional analysis with the models of rationality outlined in the foregoing. Again, when constraints of a structural character are also incorporated, the elements of a comprehensive explanatory framework begin to take shape.

Moreover, insofar as the intermediate categories of analysis are concerned, Clegg's account of the effects of managerial policy and institutional structures upon industrial relations has been crucial for delimiting the main relationships and specific variables. Thus, as will be recalled, for Clegg the structure of collective bargaining was, in most instances, shaped by "employers' organizations and managerial structure coupled with attitudes among employers. Furthermore, in his view, trade unions were "more likely to accept the methods which Marx prescribed for them, where employers play the part assigned them in the direction of the class struggle". In short, on these assumptions, managerial strategies in industrial relations have consequences not only for collective bargaining structure but also for the character of indigenous labour movements themselves.

Orientations, perception and strategy-the role of social action variables

In the context of managerial strategies, in particular, accounts of the relationship structure, institutions and social action would appear, however, to be heading for a new synthesis from the ongoing and highly fruitful interchange of propositions and analytical categories between industrial relations and industrial sociological approaches. If, on the one hand, therefore, industrial relations scholars have been seeking to broaden their theoretical compass by reference to sociological concepts, equally, sociologists have began to incorporate notions of institutions and institutionalisation into structural and action models. Nowhere has this been more in evidence than in the recent work of Gallie on international industrial relations patterns in Britain and France where a broadening of the traditional action frame of reference was undertaken without in any way introducing notions of determinism by politico-economic or technological structures. Indeed, as

Kelly has observed in this respect, whereas the action approach "effected both a methodological and a theoretical shift, away from technology, and onto orientations and perceptions. The purpose of Gallie's work... is both to examine the validity of the technological determination of attitudes, as well as to effect a further shift in perspective, away from orientations and onto institutional structures and collective strategies".

In the case in question, therefore, the pursuit of divergent industrial relations policies by British and French managers would appear to have reflected radically different cultural and institutional traditions and to have produced a variety of responses in labour-management relations themselves. Indeed, Gallie clearly recognised that 'French and British managers are products of different cultures and modes of socialisation'. Moreover, these would appear to have been reflected in disparate approaches to industrial relations with the concern of the former for *paternalism legalism* and *individualism* contrasting with the semi-constitutional strategy of British managers. Hence, while orientations and perceptions of managerial personnel were themselves clearly subject to variation, a distinctive patterning were themselves clearly as a consequence of the particular culture of the British ad French enterprises respectively. And again, as a further writer has observed, "As far as the theory of workplace organisation is concerned, this study indicates the need, previously emphasised by Clegg, for further research into the behaviour of employers and the state. For it is primarily these institutions which are responsible for shaping the accommodation structures governing industrial relations processes". In short, while action models have proved to be fundamental in introducing the notion of 'strategic choice' into the general analytical framework, the recent theoretical and empirical literature clearly suggests that these should be linked with the examination of industrial structures and cultural modes themselves.

Managerial strategy and power in industrial relations

Yet such a procedure would be far from complete without type crucial concept of power being incorporated into the general analytical matrix. After all, not only does the success or otherwise of any particular policy depend fundamentally upon the balance of power which obtains in specific enterprises; but also considerations of power would seem to inform the very genesis of distinctive strategies.

That changes in the balance of power may materially affect managerial strategies was, of course, recognised particularly by Fox in his familiar thesis that, broadly peaking, a gradual shift from 'unitary' to pluralist' perspectives in industrial relations among managerial personnel could be identified. Moreover, in *Beyond Contract* and *Man Management* the further 'radical' perspective was added as a basis for fox's own commitment to an evolving strategy for industrial relations itself. Hence, while the main elements here, what is still vital to note is how such perspectives were in large measure still vital to note is how such perspectives were in large measure conceived as reflections of shifts as power in the enterprise as economic buoyancy and the growth of welfare provisions underpinned the advance of labour up until the later 1970's. Moreover, issues of power have also been identified as basic to any understanding of the restriction of managerial strategies to pluralist notions and to the consequent rejection of radical solutions by the bulk of management and employer organizations. Similarly, as Wood and Elliott have observed in this respect, "a cursory survey of the current industrial relations scene suggests that the transition to a modified forma of pluralism, where the range of bargaining is extended to wider issues of economic regulation, will be no smoother than the earlier transition from the limited form of pluralism which acknowledged collective bargaining over wages as legitimate but rejected regulation". In short, strategic choices in industrial relations are generated in power contexts which serve partly to constrain likely outcomes but which, in some measure, are also themselves pre-selected by 'purposive' 'value' or 'system' oriented policies having implications for organizational power structure itself. Again, control exercised through the occupancy of crucial organization or institutional positions is facilitative as well as limiting since it is this capacity to transmit general decisions which provides *strategically positioned* actors with the opportunity to formulate comprehensive social choices in the first place. But as Warner has remarked: "A final overriding reason for further resolving the question of choice -v- constraints, is that he degree of power we have as citizens and/or employees depends on how far *we* have the choice to design organizations. 'Strategic choice' may well be a priority, but for whom?".

5 Dynamics of Work Group Behaviour

To this point out analysis of group behaviour in the plant and its causes has been a static one. We have identified four relatively distinctive behaviour patterns and have attempted to relate them to job configurations. But these technological factors are really *enabling conditions* They do not explain what sets off a spate of aggressive activity, what brings it to a halt, and what are the personal motivations involved. It is the dynamic problems which are the subject of this chapter. They are the intervening variables between organizational structure and group action.

Out first approach to the questions above is an examination of some of the similarities among various behaviour types. As we shall see, these comparisons suggests sharp differences in motivation between the Apathetic and Errantic groups on hand, and the Strategic and Conservative ones on the other. Also the qualities of internal leadership they find acceptable differ significantly.

Secondly, shifts in the behaviour that the groups exhibit over a period of time reveal many of the underlying forces shaping the decisions of group members. These shifts are the deviant cases that are exceptions to out general finding that behaviour patterns are stable over relatively long periods. Such unexpected and often drastic changes, as in the case of all periods of transition, are enlightening for the observer.

After summarizing our conclusions on the motivations of these groups and on the relation between their won conception of their relative power and their grievance activity, job behaviour, and selection of leadership, we turn to some consideration of the plant as a single entity. Not unexpectedly, it would appear that he total overall industrial relations climate of the plant is a function of the kinds of work groups included.

Our objectives is to move from the fine detail of the earlier chapters to larger patterns of behaviour. This procedure will enable us, in succedeeding chapters, to consider the implication of these configurations for management, for the union, and for research on work groups in industry.

Similarities and differences in group types

We have observed that there are persistent differences among work groups in their tendency to challenge management decision. More important, these differences are represented in tangible variations in the intensity and number of protest actions of one kind or another, actions which are, to an extent, apparently independent of management and union personnel and their policies.

Thus we have classified some of the work groups reported as relatively inactive; these we called our Apathetic and Conservative types. Others, which we said were the consistent hot spots or tension areas of the plants surveyed, we termed the Erratic and STrategic groups. Interestingly, however, the dividing line most sharply defined by the data is not the one separating the highly active self-interest groups from the relatively inactive, passive ones. It is the behaviour patterns of the Apathetic and Erratic groups which basically are similar. In parallel, the behaviour patterns of the Strategic and the Conservative groups also have much in common.

The behaviour of the apathetic-erratic axis

The groups whose behaviour places them in the Apathetic-Erratic categories seem much more *personal* in their relationship with management and the union. They are not seeking any long-run readjustments in their relative economic and prestige position in the plant. Rather, they usually are attending to preserve their customary rights. Theirs is a holding operation, usually much less involved with the use of the union as pressuring agent than other more "far-seeing" work groups.

Because the expectations of the Apathetic-Erratic groups are often not made explicit, compared to the insistent demands of the more premeditative groups, their reactions to management moves are often unpredictable. Further, such reactions are likely to be the product of real frustration. There is a high emotional content in their dependence upon customary relations with supervision and their desire to preserve the status quo. When these conditions are "violated," the reaction can be sudden and violent. When the members of these groups are convinced that their "way of life" is threatened they will fight back as savagely, if not ore so, as the group that in a calculating way is seeking some new benefit or right.

This need to preserve customary relations is difficult to make explicit. The protests of these groups seldom center on specific overt violations of contractual agreements, or if they do, their real causes are not recognized by managements, or if they do, their real causes are not recognized by management and the union. Therefore, such grievances may continue and grow, and when the break comes it s more likely to be sudden and explosive because of pent-up dissatisfaction. The grievance procedure, whatever its structure, has failed to drain off the frustrations. Often there will be an element of contagion throughout the process, the overt expression of dissatisfaction spreading among those most susceptible to it.

The groups which lack the cohesion required for careful advance planning and the patience born of bargaining skill often find themselves in a box of their own making. They rashly commit themselves to abrupt and illegal action; then when management or the union threatens reprisals, they have no organizational means to back down and still save face. Thus many of their aggressive activities may be the result of the frustration created by their own actions, which have closed all excitable retreats or means of escape.

Paradoxically, the most discouraging aspect of the position of the Apathetic and Erratic groups in th plant is the likelihood that they will provide the most serious opposition to technological change. Although the Apathetics offer minimum open challenges to management, their attitude, as well as that of the Erratics, is a blind resistance to what is new and different. They lack the internal organization and structure which would provide them with the capacity for change. To be sure, innovation can be imposed upon them, but as individuals they remain convinced that they have been seriously injured and the results will be calamitous. Thus their output often suffers for extended periods, not because of a concerted slowdown, but because the individual employee is sure that his job has been made much more difficult, and unfairly so.

The behaviour of the conservative- strategic axis

In contrast to the behaviour described above, we have seen that many work groups are more legalistically inclined. They have learned, particularly since the advent of the union, to think in contract terms, and they are ever ready to check management's conformity with the literal meaning of that document.

At times they are satisfied, being assured by the computation that they are doing "all right." But more often, particularly for those groups in the middle that we have called Strategic, the old doubts remain that "we are not getting all to which we are entitled." As long as these doubts continue, pressure will be applied at every conceivable opportunity which promises the chance of getting more for themselves.

Most of their legalistic grievances are well thought through and well expressed. There is little likelihood of sudden explosion, because both management and the members understand their demands. Their very ability to communicate these wants increases the chance of their being satisfied or out in another way, decreases the possibility of any sudden explosion. Management can predict with a fair degree of accuracy when the mild pressure of these groups will be purposefully converted into more serious concerted demonstrations.

In turn, because they can be bargained with, agreement of the introduction of change in the groups can be more readily, although not painlessly, obtained. Their is not blind resistance to innovation. Therefore, when "sold," they will completely adopt and adapt to the new circumstances rather than engage in either extended passive resistance or pitched battles.

Another way of looking at this distinction between the Erratic-Apathetic groups on the one hand and the Strategic-Conservative groups on the other is suggested by Gouldner in his report on a wildcat strike. He contrasts "the `traditionalists' who were custom rooted sought a restoration of the past.... with the `market men' who sought formal recognition of *new* rights and obligations... emphasized the pecuniary implications of workers' grievances.."

His intensive analysis of a single plant appears to be consistent with the finding of this study.

Variations in type of informal leader selected

In an important sense, the leadership qualities of the informal leader, through whom the interest group deals with management and union are the crucial link between potential action and action taken. The leader does not himself determine the actions of his group; the group will tend to select an individual whose characteristics suit their unique temperament. Our vidual whose characteristics suit their unique temperament. Our data in this area are only suggestive, since we has little contact with these men and descriptions of their behaviour were highly incomplete, It would appear, however, that there is a significant relationship between the personality type that appeals to a groups and the kind of group involved.,

Apathetic groups and, to a lesser extent, Erratic groups frequently seemed to permit the leadership function to gravitate to highly aggressive individuals with a strong need to dominate the situation, both within the group and in group relations with management and the union. These individuals would tolerate to competition for the center of the stage; they has to have the last word in every encounter. Most interesting, and certainly most unexpected from the point of view of many management officials, was the readiness with which these leaders could on occasion transfer their censorious focus from he company to the rank and file. Even while describing their role in precipitating a wildcat strike or a serious verbal attack on the company, they might comment that the company was making a mistake in not promoting them into the personnel department! Needless to say, their belief that such staff men have the authority to impose their point of view on the employees makes it seem clear that theirs was not a rebellion against authority but, rather, a highly aggressive need to demonstrate authority and to work within an authoritarian framework.

The social scientist might describe these kinds of people as "charistmatic" leaders. Their striking and appealing personality characteristics, the uniqueness which sets them apart form their colleagues, makes them the obvious choice of those groups that wish to be dominated, or better, wish to follow a "spellbinder".

In contrast it would appear that Strategic and Conservative groups selected individuals who temperamentally were much more suited to responding to the initiations of the group. The group, being able to demonstrate a consensus toward problems, utilized as an external leader someone who would do their bidding and would not go off on his own. In fact they would reject the leadership attempts of members within their own groups whom they considered overbearing, irrespo-nsible, or dangerous.

Such leaders were much less flashy. Although they might be intellectually committed to an antimanagement bias and determined to press certain grievances with all the vigour they possessed, they did not seem to demonstrate aggressiveness for the sake of being aggressive. Their hostilities expressed themselves in controlled convictions, not emotional outbursts. As such, they were much easier to negotiate with, and when one such leader was promoted to a management position he was likely to do a good job of supervision. This situation contrasted with the showing of the charismatic leaders developed in Apathetic and Erratic groups, who, after appointment to supervisory positions, often incurred the enmity of employees because of their autocratic approach to the job of managing.

Shifts in group behaviour over time

Our analysis to this point has been concerned with the static elements in work group behaviour. We have been primarily interested in examining group behaviour and in turn relating it to plant technology.

Actually we have already departed to some extent from this static picture by describing two kinds of cases where relatively short-run shifts take place. We observed a number of instances when Erratic groups shifted dramatically to Apathetic, in almost miraculous "conversions". Overnight, sometimes. A contentious trouble spot became cooperative and peaceful. This event might often, or to unknown internal changes. what was significant about the conversions, however, was the rapidity with which they took place, seemingly much faster than any basic morale change could work itself out. Just as quickly such a group might shirt back to the offensive, and with no greater provocation than has previously occurred.

Although we have no definite evidence on this possibility, it is likely that the susceptibility of these groups to the influence of a stranger, to which we referred earlier, may be partially responsible for the conversion phenomenon. A newly introduced troublemaker or a newly elected steward who believes in a more disciplined department can affect the group with unusual swiftness.

Similarly in the case of Conservative groups, we noted several instances where previous inactivity has placed them at a disadvantage in the scale of plant benefits. For a short period they then responded like Strategic groups, charging forward simultaneously on many fronts to pressure management to make concessions. When the battle was won, however, they usually returned to their former inactive status. Nevertheless, their conversions were not the sudden shifts characteristic of Erratic groups, but rather the result of a gradual recognition that they have fallen behind in plant benefits

Let us now examine two longer-run shifts.

Structurally, the group fits clearly into our Strategic category. Although the jobs are individual and have close tolerance, they are in no sense a skilled craft requiring a long training period. In this work a number of operators are concentrated in one geographic location, and they are replaceable; current broach operators cannot easily find similar work outside the plant. Yet the behaviour of out group was typically that of a Conservative group. They were no longer pushing for new benefits, and legalistic grievances were a rarity. They has won an unambiguous position of secure respect and assured benefits, and were responding with true *noblesse oblige*.

Even though we think we can explain these two shifts, there remain a number of unresolved questions. The reader will recall the observation of union representative, that the metal polishers in one plant lost their strength when management scattered their operation among a number of departments. Yet we have observed many groups with substantial economic strength whose operations are scattered. However, the latter groups have not experienced any change; inspectors, for example, have always been located in widely separated locations.

In the automobile industry the trimmers have not suffered any apparent decrease in their ability to exert concerted pressure, although they suffered a serious technological blow when stapling and new materials rendered unnecessary some of their upholstering skills. Why did they not suffer the same fate as the grinders described above? One difference may be that the trimmers' change in the automobile industry did not result in decreased job opportunities for the men involved. Thus, their strength was about sapped by internal squabbles over who should retain job rights.

Explanations such as these are not satisfactory, however. We need to know much more about the conditions under which pressure groups change their behaviour patterns. All we are able to do at this point in our research is to suggest which kinds of shifts are most likely to occur.

It should be noted that the short-run shifts take place within the two major constellations: Apathetic-Erratic and Strategic-Conservative, not between them.

Group goals and motivations

In Most of out discussion up to this point we have been interested in examining persistent differences in group behaviour rather than in explaining the motivation of the members responsible for any given pattern of action. To be sure, we have made reference to very general kinds of goals, such as the maintenance or improvement of economic benefit levels share by the members of the interest group. However such explanations are rather inadequate, particularly when we begin discussing the shifts undergone by some groups as described previously. At this stage, then, we want to summarize out knowledge of group goals. There is a direct interrelation between the plant environment and work group behaviour that we can point to as having some significance in setting off certain chain reactions. At least three distinct influences on work group goals can be distinguished:

1. Intraplant comparisons of benefits one group enjoys to those others are receiving.
2. Some direct threat to security emanating usually, but not exclusively, from management.
3. As a function of the previous success or failure of the group in responding to 1 and /or 2.

Let us explore each of these factors briefly.

Intraplant comparisons

We have already observed that high activity is associated with a somewhat ambiguous prestige position. Work groups in the upper middle ranges of skill and earnings have met some of the criteria which justifies in their eyes, if not in management's view, pay and working conditions "almost" comparable to those enjoyed by the recognized top skilled personnel. As we noted in the case of the hand screw machine operators, these middle-range workers expect to be much better off than those they see as being *below* them in importance, and almost as well off as those they recognize as being *above* them in job skills. They utilize the same reference groups to establish their skill level, seizing upon one criterion, such as the fineness of the tolerance for the work they ar doing, and excluding others which do not support their case.

We have referred to special interest groups because these groups have particular economic goals: securing better work standards, greater protection in the case of technological change, higher hourly rates, more overtime, looser incentive standards, and so on. Each of the goals has a *comparative* aspect: better than, greater than, higher than, looser than, more than the conditions or status of some other group.

The plant grapevine carries general impressions as to how hard various groups work for approximately what general order of income-although the accuracy of these impressions leaves much to be desired. Actually we know very little about how these comparisons are made, and need to know much more before generalizing on how a group decides it is being paid equitably or inequitably.

The economist has stressed interplant comparisons as the dynamic fore in the labor market. We would suggest that with the impact of seniority, retirement, job guarantees, and the protections of unionization, the internal labor market becomes an equally important determinant of worker behaviour.

An interesting example of the effect of "other work groups" was furnished by a steelworker official. He observed that foundries are often hot sports, highly aggressive in seeking fullfilment of their demands *when they are part of larger manufacturing organizations*. However, when the plant is entirely devoted to the foundry operation, they are relatively weak and inactive.

We might speculate that in these more diversified plants the position of the foundry is ambiguous. Earnings are high to compensate for the difficult working conditions, the work is heavy, and more recently there has been a serious conditions, the work is heavy, and more recently there has been a serious shortage of applicants for this kind of work; but the reputation of the foundry is very low among other employees, who tend to look down on foundry workers because of the hot, dirty, heavy work they perform.

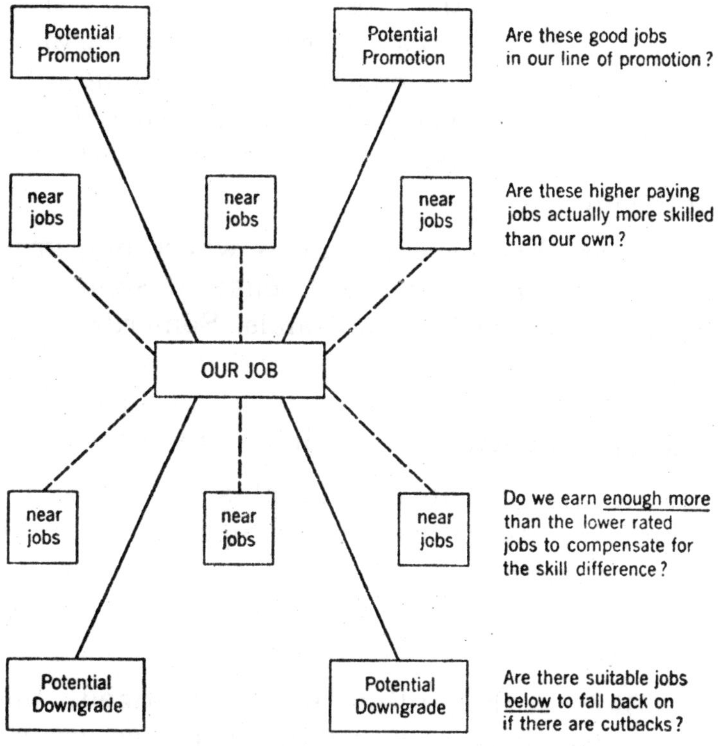

The economic world of the worker in his work group

Our study of the decision-making process in local unions concluded that there are many areas subject to collective bargaining in which one group gains relatively more that another. There are other group demands which can only be satisfied at the direct expense of some other work group. For the former case a typical example is the negotiation of specific job rates:

Whenever the union officers obtain improved earnings for one group they reduce the relative prestige of other workers. The elimination of what are inequities in the eyes of one group may create inequities in the eyes of a competing department. ... Whenever the union initiaties or acquiesces to change affecting job evaluation or incentive rates it runs the risk of upsetting *customary differentials*.

Then there are instances where one group must lose, in an absolute sense, If some other groups is to gain its demands. Seniority issues division of retroactive pay, and decisions where work within the plant is to be performed are relevant examples of the win-lose pattern.

In all of these examples one group is comparing its gains from unionization with the gains of another group. In fact, the introduction of the union often increases the importance of these rivalries:

Before the union was organized, poor communications made it difficult for one group to compare itself with another. Information about weekly paychecks, hours worked, seniority, and all the rest could be passed from group to group only by means of rumors and personal friendships.

The unions have opened new channels of communication. Contract requirements that seniority lists and job vacancies be posted create a wealth of opportunities for workers to compare their positions in the plant. Job workers are now sensitive to cost-of-living indices, they know what the other guys are getting and how hard they work for it."

Finally, by providing a grievance procedure which channels worker complaints into ares where something can and often is done about them, the union encourages the development of intergroup comparisons.

External threat

Secondly, a threat to a group's existing benefits level may stimulate the members to action. This is the motivation analyzed in much of the research on informal group behaviour in industry.

We have suggested that threats to the exiting status quo are more important for Apathetic and Erratic groups which tend to react spontaneously than for the groups which are more legalistically oriented. However, even for the latter groups, some threat in the current situation may be the initial motivating factor to convert a potentially active group into a consistently aggressive one. As Caplow suggests, there may be an optimum level of threat which "jells" the group into an action-oriented unit. Tasting success, they remain active, although the original threat has disappeared. however, their goal is no longer a return to normalcy, but, rather, is directed toward improvement.

Perhaps there should be a special category called "obsolescence groups." Managements report that certain groups whose technological importance has declined drastically are never-ending sources of grievances. The trimmers whose skill with the tack hammer has been replaced by the use of stapling guns may be a good case in point. Certain foundry occupations similarly have lost their skill requirements and are focal points for trouble.

Where the threat is too imposing, the result can be demoralization. As we have noted, there are many instances where reduced work opportunities resulted in serious internal bickerings over seniority and in differences with the union which destroyed an active group.

Relations of group power to its level of activity

By implication, at least, we have been talking about this third variable: How much does the level of aggressive activity depended on the inherent *power* residing within the group? We might easily assume that power which insures successful group efforts would encourage still greater efforts. After pressuring for an easier work standard and winning it, we might expect to find further incentive to repeat this behaviour. Surely the psychologists with their law of Effect would predict: behaviour that is rewarded tends to be repeated. A British economist has observed: "If there is one thing which can be more damaging to the orderly conduct of industrial relations than an unofficial strike, it is a successfully unofficial strike."

We know more bout the negative situation; it is easier to observe. The failure of a group to achieve an objective, particularly when the failure can be attributed to internal faults in organization, reduced the incentive to try again.

One department sought to gain a premium payment for a holiday eve or, preferably, time off without pay when production quotas for the period has already been met. They noted that other departments did not have night work before a holiday. When management refused, the men agreed among themselves to stay home on the night concerned and then claim to have been ill. When the shift reported the following evening, half of the members learned that the other half has been on the job the previous night. After that fiasco, suggestions that the group try other pressure tactics, such as a slowdown to obtain a looser incentive standard, were always greeted with the risk my neck so that someone else can go behind my back and cut my throat for me?"

In another case reported by the author, the failure of just that kind of endeavor was instrumental in discouraging group efforts for some years. In that department, a number of senior workers ignored an agreement to turn in less production as a means of contesting new production standards.

It would seem reasonable for a group to take into account its *chances for success* before pushing ahead with a protest. We expect that the group's "experience rating" of their own power would condition their protests of shop conditions. It has been suggested that groups that have experienced the effectiveness of their power are more likely to see "poor" working conditions, "tight" standards, "tough" supervision, etc., as correctable.

Of course, success breeds success in other ways as well. Members' attraction to a group, and the loyalty they are willing to demonstrate toward it varies directly with the prestige accorded the group. When successes are forthcoming, the attachment becomes stronger. Conversely, failures weaken identification, and persistent failures may result in the individuals complete severance of all ties with his work group. We have observed instances where employees applied for transfers out of departments which they saw as lacking influence in plant affairs and suffering thereby. Many times key leaders and prestige figures are lost in the members' rush to find a safer haven within a group that is more powerful in defending its interests.

However, we have also seen that there may be an end, or at least a temporary halt to the spiral-success-new demands-more success, etc. Although we do not believe in the concept of the static equilibrium which, once reached, shuts off further demands, there are cases where a group places itself in such a preferred position that there is little incentive for further activity. A shift of behaviour pattern from Strategic to Conservative would be an illustration. Such a transformation is probably due in part to management's own change of attitude concerning the group. The company learns to anticipate the probable reaction of employees before acting, thus "protecting" the group from hardship. This is more likely to be the case with respect to Conservative groups that have a high replacement value than to Strategic groups which often appear to be more expendable.

Finally, in this consideration of the relation between power and activity, we have observed that serious intergroup frictions may be a contributing cause of some serious outbursts against management because:

1. Under some circumstances, the members of the group may find it acceptable to express their frustrations over interpersonal frictions in antimanagement grievances. This action provides an aggressive outlet and also serves to assuage any feelings to guilt over their failure to be normal and to like one another as members of the same family.
2. There will be times when internal differences make it impossible even to express a grievance that represents a consensus. The group is in disagreement, not agreement, over what needs "righting". As a result, the normal and peaceful workings of the grievance procedure do not drain off the problems. Rather, a substantial backlog of unsolved and often unexpressed dissatisfaction accumulates, until the inevitable explosion occurs.

Here we have a rather fine distinction. Those unsuccessful in utilizing group pressures to win improved benefits for themselves are more likely to accept certain elements of their working life as inevitable, elements that the more successful groups might be willing to challenge. However, these same unsuccessful groups have a low level of tolerance for many petty threats from management. Lacking nay assurance that they have enough control in the situation to win out eventually, they may explode, almost spontaneously-at times when they think they see an inequity coming.

On the other hand, where self-confidence has been built up over time with the recognition that "we do swing some weight around here," petty annoyances and fears can be tolerated. As we have noted, prolonged negotiations and pressure tactics require patience and restraint. Overt pressures must be saved for the more important cases.

In the same way, a threat to an important group benefit can galvanize its members to action. rarely is the threat completely dissipated, and even if it is, the success experience may be all that is needed to teach the employees involved that converted action is rewarding.

Power begets power-once this lesson is learned it is likely to be repeated. The prestige that groups gain both from the benefits they win, and from their success in winning them, provides a further impetus for continued activity.

Another way of assessing these relationships is to look for a moment at dissatisfaction. We have really been saying that there are two kinds of grievances. On the one hand, we have the major long-run problems of relative plant status. Here a group is attempting to carve out a more permanent and dissatisfactory position for itself, in terms of relative earnings and working conditions. It may never achieve what it accepts as success, but the process of "carving out" in itself provides a feeling of success or failure. Superimposed on the pattern of major problems are the minor day-to-day irritations: an employee is disciplined harshly; a shortage of parts reduces incentive earnings; work is shifted to another department; and so on. Some of these groups-the obsolescent ones-are attacking what are essentially insoluble problems; others have literally lifted themselves by their bootstraps and are for the present "at peace with the world"; some are in midstream in what could easily be a decade-long struggle to improve their job; and some have given up in defeat.

Power, satisfaction, and productivity

It is a long step to move from observations of group behaviour to questions of morale and productivity. these factors are much less tangible and less observable, but certainly no less important. We have already implied that the expressions of aggression on the part of some groups often do not involve any increase in satisfaction. The immediate target is but a "last straw" following a whole series of unresolved and often unexpressed grievances. But what about the highly legalistic groups that know what they want, and presumably know how to get it? We surmise that the groups having effective power do experience increased satisfaction. Management was likely to comment, in answer to outer questions about these groups, that, although they has many grievances they were not necessarily poor workers. similarly, turnover did not seem to be a problem here as it did in many of the less consistently active departments. Our third basic of appraisal, still an indirect one, was in terms of the leadership of these groups. Over and over management representatives described the informal leaders of these groups as "excellent workers," slated for promotion," and "conscientous workmen". This was not often the case where the group's behaviour has been Erratic or Apathetic. Their leaders were more likely to be unsatisfactory employees.

Although such evaluations are certainly subject to serious bias, it is significant that workers whose "troublemaking" and "unjustified grievances" were resented, could still be seen as productive and efficient. We would have expected quite the opposite result.

Dr. George Strauss in an unpublished study of two groups of insurance salesmen observes that high grievance activity and high productivity were positively correlated. Most string was the fact that the high grievance group was also most vocal in criticizing management and supporting union penalties against strikebreakers and employees who appeared to be "to friendly" to the company during a period of hostile union-management relations. Nevertheless, they outproduced all of their more loyal colleagues.

Our own conclusion is that in the long run, the worker's confidence in his ability to protect himself and to secure equitable treatment is essential to satisfactory morale and eventually to productivity itself. Many of the so-called legalistic groups undoubtedly enjoyed this high level of group confidence and group power. The same situation facilitated an efficient and systematic method of resolving conflicts; grievances did not fester. Viewed over a short period of time their perception of a need to pressure management or the union might result in production blockages. Over a longer period of time, however, they would tend to be above average in effort expended on management goals. Put in another way, successful *upward* initiations releases productivity.

The same factors would contribute to a more healthy relationship with the union. Such groups would be likely to support and take some responsibility for the leadership of that organization. As we shall consider in a later section, this positive attitude can be of major significance to the entire plant's system of industrial relations.

Researchers in industrial relations have been overlay impressed with the workers' need for *social* satisfactions on the job. Undoubtedly there is truth in Mayo's observations on the mule-spinning department of a textile plant: isolated workmen become obsessive and less productive, and these conditions improve when the opportunity for social interaction is provided. It is significant however that Mayo later modified his original hypothesis to take into account the effect of the *change itself* on worker attitudes; that is, he recognized that management's willingness to make changes that improved working conditions was interpreted as a favorable sing by the workers and was in part responsible for their increased efforts.

Of equal importance in encouraging productivity may be the factor of *experiencing group solidarity and success in attaining economic satisfaction* . In a number of the studies of the Survey Research Center, "pride in work group" is one of the major correlates, and one of the few consistent correlates of high productivity. It is not unreasonable to assume that groups develop such pride, in part, out of the experience of unity and successes in pursuing common objectives. We have seen many instances of the reverse, where failure to develop satisfactory cohesion resulted in mutual recriminations. On the other hand, the *esprit de corps* of a group that has proven itself in a difficult grievance case is noteworthy. There is real satisfaction in the experience of having maintained unity under trying circumstances to win a difficult objective.

The total plant as an environmental factor

Also to be taken into account in explaining the industrial relations climate of a plant is the total structure of that organization, not only that of the constituent departments or work units.

Plants which are primarily assembly or line operations or where crew activities predominate seemed to be very different in their climate of industrial relations from plants in which individual or batch operations were the dominant structure. Pendent plants, which lacked strong, individual operation work groups with some status, comprised the polar cases in the sample. Among them were numbered the very best-and the worst-industrial relations records. These plants seemed to have more than their share of union-management cooperation and/or complete absence of conflict, and also more than their share of situations where the union ran rampant, and where they were constantly threatened by irresponsible strike activity. The other plants with more individual operations departments were rarely as good or as bad in the matter of industrial relations; they clustered in geneous concentrations of single jobs, were similar to assembly-line plants in occupying polar positions.

Our own explanation of this contrast is admittedly speculative and tentative. We propose this hypothesis: Where the plant lacks strong occupationally oriented work groups, the union leader tends to be more independent of the members' judgment and feelings. This independence can result in the development of highly cooperative relationships with management, relationship which might be doomed to failure in other situations where the prejudices and fears of specific rank and file groups would cause the overthrow of any officer who was too much in the good graces of management. However, this can be a highly dangerous situation for management as well, for it may explain those instances where a small officer clique dominates the plant and irresponsibly creates ceaseless turmoil.

We suggest, furthermore, that where work groups are well organized internally they demand the constant attention of the union leadership. The latter must be able to respond to the grievances and feelings of such groups in a manner that may make real union-management cooperation difficult, if not impossible. The selfishness of the individual work groups may prevent concessions where each makes a sacrifice for the greater good of all. However, such groups are also excellent "watch dogs". The union leadership cannot steer an antonomous course, creating strife for purely personal or political objectives. These groups are too conscious of their economic needs to permit a situation to deteriorate, as some we have observed, so that management eventually abandoned the plant because of the impossibility of insuring continuous, economic production.

It should be noted that there is a distinction between local unions which must respond to the demands of several strongly united interest groups and locals completely dominated by a single interest group. There were only one or two cases in our sample which appeared to be in the latter category. Unfortunately it was nuclear as to what the longer run effects of such domination by a single group might be. Our impression, however, was that this was a somewhat unstable condition, although the union-management pattern was similar to the situation where no single group had that much power.

We are suggesting that open conflict situations often reflect the inability of the rank and file to make themselves heard. They lack the stable group strength that could permit them to control the union. The leadership then, not necessarily because of planned malevolence, but because of lack of membership checks, becomes a group apart. Where it is comprised of highly aggressive personalities the results can be continuous and destructive strife. When the membership is not able to control the leadership, the union may be running rampant without actually satisfying the basic dissatisfaction of the members. In fact the frustrations involved, particularly the loss of earnings due to strikes and slowdowns, may only aggravate the employees and serve as fertile ground for still more unsatisfying demonstrations.

We received information about at least one well publicized case of union-management cooperation where the union functioned as a highly autonomous unit. After a period, management became concerned with the long-run problems of having a union leadership that took so much initiative in turning down member grievances and jointly administering a new production standards programs. Unlike most of the locals we has studied previously, which has learned through painful experience the value of shying away from joint responsibility for unpopular decisions, these leaders activity sought out new situations in which they could share the authority role with management.

While many managements might consider this a utopian situation, where the union takes such responsibility for imposing relatively unpleasant decisions on it membership, the company in question discovered that this paradise has its disadvantages. The union functioned less successfully as a communication channel to management; serious sources of discontent were not systematically being uncovered, and often the company has to take the initiative in ferreting out the sources of what were obviously serious problems which the union has squelched. In return for the union assuming management functions, the company recognized that they has to assume certain union responsibilities.

There is... the case in which union officials and members of management achieve a good adjustment and an equilibrium as a result of a much higher frequency of interaction with each other than that which the union leaders have with their members.... These weaknesses, the result of the relations of union leaders to management, show the necessity of a careful definition of these relations so that the union *can operate as a compensatory mechanism* and thus reduce the disturbances in the factory and increases the morale of its members.

Chapple also concludes that union officials in conflict situations, by increasing their initiations to members of the rank and file when they themselves are under pressure from management, become very much "like the first line supervisors in the company". Thus a vicious circle is created in these plants where day-to-day problems do not work themselves out through the grievance process. The leaders, lacking strong group support and thus failing to get management to move, begin pressuring the rank and file for more activity. To the membership this just adds to the burden of downward pressures already coming from their supervisors, and the result is a more disturbed, lower morale group of employees. The grievance process fails to work in these types of plants as a compensatory mechanism.

All this would cause one to conclude that there is a delicate balance in the relation of union leaders to their members and to management. Only in certain well prescribed situations, such as some of those described above, will the presence of the union serve to improve overall employee morale and serve as a stabilizing force within the plant community.

New forms of technology, such as the methods associated with automation, may serve to break up established groups and fragment the social structure of the plant, In many plants the trend towards more continuous work-flow systems, increasing differentiation of work, and greater number of subgroupings of employees clearly foretells drastic shifts in the industrial relations of the organization.

Profitability. Another total plant factor, the significance of which is somewhat difficult to evaluate, is the profitability variable. There is some evidence that in marginal operations management is more likely to turn to the union for help in improving productivity. they may also be less resistant to individual or group demands for concessions under threats of slowdowns and stoppages. In critical situation, therefore the power of some of these groups may be magnified the economic distress of the firm. In the highly profitable, successful operation, management can afford to be more independent and resistant to such encroachment. In turn, this resistance reduces somewhat the influence of the stronger work groups.

We really need to know more about the "laws of combination" pertaining to these concerted interest groups. What is the difference in the effect of having *one* as compared to several groups with a reputation for high concerted activity in the pant? For example, we observed in plants with limited numbers of such groups, departments such as toolrooms, inspectors, and materials handlers, which otherwise might be overshadowed, become more highly active.

It is possible to distinguish among plants on the basis of the kind of group that is the most active in challenging management and the union. Thus in any given plant at a given time, the real hot spots or groups. We have seen situations where the highly legalistic groups in the plant is the focus for industrial relations problems. In other situations the less predictable, Erratic work teams are the source of periodic, if not continuous, plant turmoil. It is also conceivable that some groups we have categorized as Conservative would renew their aggressive activity after a quiescent period as a result of finding themselves in a relatively worse economic position because of the greater political efforts made by other groups. The conclusion of their industrial relations climate.

Further exploration of the relationship between the overall technology of the plant and the behaviour of various work groups and the union should provide a fruitful field of additional research. At the moment at least, out observations certainly do not qualify as conclusions. they only suggest the potential value of future research.

6 Managers, Industrial Democracy and Control

Insofar as the general categories of social action are concerned, managerial strategies of social responsibility have been conventionally analysed in terms of Wertrational conduct in which moral and idealistic-evaluative aspects have been uppermost, while payment systems clearly belong to the domain of Zweckrational action in which predominantly utilitarian-conative elements and an appeal to material interests may be discerned. Turning, them, to the question of industrial democracy and employee participation both these pure types of social action may be identified in experiments in this sphere, since, even though certain departures have been established as a means informed by the managerial commitment to specific Zweckrational objectives. And, as a consequence, it is scarcely surprising that, by and large, mangers' own policies for employee participation have been designed to ensure that their capacity to shape, say, commercial or technical issues has remained intact, while actual practices have been supported only conditionally upon the accomplishment of greater efficiency, adaptability and flexibility coupled with improvements in the climate of industrial relations itself.

The primary aim of this chapter, then, is to undertaken conceptual analysis of managerial policies concerning industrial democracy and employee participation by focusing, above all, upon the actual effects perhaps controversially, we shall seek to reinforce the case argued elsewhere that partly as a result of the high total control vested in the organization by participate initiatives and partly because the manager has almost invariably been the principal beneficiary of any political movement towards decentralised industrial influence of managerial personnel has rarely been circumscribed by historical and contemporary transformations of this nature. But before embarking upon such a review, it is incumbent upon us to clarify a number of central premises and to examine the background factors which help to elucidate the move towards democratic administrative forms in the first place. This will then constitute a basis for an explanatory account of the objectives and consequences of industrial democracy for mangers in a variety of enterprises and establishments.

Definitions and measures

"Research on participation", as Nightingale has argued, "is entering a new era". After all, while in the early human relations tradition the types of participation which were advocated took place "with the existing hierarchical structure of the organization", recently there has emerged "a growing interest in forms of participation that are based on a substantial redistribution of power to organization members at lower hierarchical levels". Yet for the purposes of this inquiry two fundamental questions arise, the first concerning the commitments of managers to the reforms themselves and the second the experiences of these managerial personnel in fully fledged institutional experiments. Moreover, although our knowledge of the effects of the various programmes upon managerial groups is still not of a sufficient order to permit definitive conclusions, equally, a wide range of researches have enabled a sharp definition of the main hypotheses. Indeed, the bulk of the evidence now clearly points to the view that far from occasioning a serious demise in the overall power and influence of managerial personnel, the expansion of democratic practices has been associated with a general augmentation of the total control of the establishment's members as a whole.

Nevertheless, it is difficult to shed light on the effects of participative government upon managers without prior definition of key concepts and an evaluation of those measurement dimensions which are obviously basic to empirical researches. Industrial democracy, then, has conventionally been understood to imply an exercise of power or influence by workers and their representatives over decisions within their places of employment. Nonetheless although the diffusion of this idea and its institutionalisation has been genuinely worldwide; equally, as the international labour office has recorded, there are a wide range of formulae "from workers' self management to collective bargaining, including workers' councils and workers' representation on managerial bodies, and extending to the workplace level where workers are associated with the determination of the manner in which their jobs are carried out". The institutions of industrial democracy are thus ones of great complexity; a situation which not only reflects the considerable intricacies of internal structure and diversity of origin but also the varied experience of managerial personnel within each principal type.

But insofar as industrial democracy and employee participation are concerned managerial strategies and the actual effects of given experiments upon the managers themselves cannot be fully understood without reference to four main themes. These cover first, the distinctions between control, authority, power and influence; second, the levels in the managerial hierarchy; third, the range of issues; and fourth, the scope of involvement in the decision in question.

In principles, then, formal control and the legitimate sources of enterprise authority undergo transformations in broad encompassing programmes foe employee participation (e.g. co-determination and especially workers' self-management). In such cases, not only are the personnel who are represented upon strategic decision making committees markedly different from the pervious membership but also their constituencies (to which, in the last analysis, their allegiances are owed) also change. But even on a priority grounds it is far from axiomatic that the power of mangers i.e. the probability that managers will be in a position to carry out their will despite resistance or their influence (i.e. the capacity to ensure actions concordant with objectives) are so dramatically altered by the experiments of this nature or, of course, that in the more limited managerially-initiated programmes, that there are major losses along any of these key dimensions of the 'power vocabulary' whatsoever. Again, if we deploy the familiar definition of influence of French, Israel and As "a process in which two or more persons influence each other involving certain plans, policies and decisions" then clearly, as Strauss has remarked, joint decision making processes in themselves provide only the opportunity and not the guarantee of influence over key issues in the establishments in question.

Moreover, it is clear that the structural location of the managers themselves varies in Western societies and in Eastern European state socialist countries, in public and private enterprises in any given country, and in large scale joint stock enterprises (in which the overt influence of shareholders may be minimal) and the family firm with perhaps a few hundred employees, Again, the distinctions between director and manager, between personnel at different levels in the managerial hierarchy, and between "cosmopolitan" managers with skills anchored in professional associates and their more "local" counterparts in the line hierarchy may all the fundamental importance in producing different social experiences which in turn engender variations in outlook and behaviour not least on the question of industrial democracy itself. In short, the levels of involvement and decision making influence of a number of groups both within and external to the organization can differ considerably, the Industrial Democracy in Europe researchers listing first line supervisors, middle management, top management, levels above the establishment, permanent representatives bodies at the establishment level, and bodies in institutions outside of company or establishment. By the same token, in seeking to determine the precise impact of managerial personnel in the democratically administered enterprise it is essential to incorporate measures of issues actually influenced or controlled by the various members of the organization. Hence, for the purposes of measurement, in the IDE study short, middle and long-term decisions were deployed, while as strauss has insisted, "subject matter and organizational level are connected. Autonomous work-groups, for example, are concerned with operational details, i.e. with means, while company-wide co-determination is concerned with strategic decisions and means". Again, although the IDE study revealed the significance of legislative intervention for actual practice (dejure participative structures were found to be "a better guide than contextual variables of both worker influence and involvement"; equally, there are still analytical distinctions between what the same investigators have referred to as (1) dejure patterns and structures, (2) the distribution of influence and (3) patterns of involvement. Meanwhile, in the Decision Organizations survey, strategic, tactical and operational decisions were all separated for theoretical and empirical purposes respectively.

Finally, the scope of influence exerted by managers over given issues can differ considerably, the degree of variation being measured by the so-called influence-power continuum. As it happens a number of such dimensions have surfaced in the literature to date, but the DIO investigation incorporated no information, information, opportunities to give advice, advice taken into consideration, joint decision making and complete control. Moreover, in this context it is worth mentioning the extent to which, even in non participatory organizations, the influence of middle managers has been shown to be of only limited magnitude.

(2) The genesis of industrial democracy institutions and the role of managers

The analytical, and empirical significance of these definitions and distinctions will become apparent throughout this chapter but first of all it is of course vital to locate more specific discussions on the role of managers in the emerging institutions of industrial democracy within broader frameworks concerning the general development of the phenomenon itself. Nonetheless, it is by no means easy to identify the major "causative" variables here unless there is some prior indication of the main schools of thought and their central points of variation. By way of clarifying these cardinal issues, then we may appropriately delineate the following principal perspectives:-

Integrative models

A. Structural based on the concept of system integration-institutionalisation of conflict themes

B. Subjective based on the concept of social integration

   (i) A solution to anomie

   (ii) Bureaucracy and democracy associated with processes of rationalisation

   (iii)Spread of concept or citizenship into employment relations

Disjunctive models

A. Structural

   (i) Marxian and marxisant

   (ii) Other conflict approaches

B. Subjective

   (i) Rising expectations

   (ii) Alienation

   (iii)'Political' struggles extended into work roles and relationships

Integrative models

In the first place, therefore, there is a fundamental distinction between those perspectives on industrial democracy in which the sharing of industrial decision making power is viewed as bringing about a reconciliation of interests and objectives between management and worker and those in which, by way of contrast, no long term accommodation along these lines is deemed possible. Nonetheless, there are a number of variants within each school that in turn may be classified into structural and subjective approaches respectively. Moreover, in the first general category the respective divisions roughly correspond with Lockwood's distinction between system and social integration; the first embracing the notion of a structural reconciliation of interests via the institutionalization of industrial democracy and the second covering social group and normative integration occasioned by participative modes of governance themselves.

The institutionalization of conflict thesis gained general currency in sociological and industrial relations circles in the 1950's and early 1960's but seemed less than apposite as disruptions in industry began to escalate during the subsequent years. Nonetheless there is still widespread anticipation among advocates of industrial democracy that the divisions among social classes and among position in the labour process could be diminished if not wholly attenuated by such institutional arrangements, as indeed was propounded in the bullock report itself. "It is our belief that the way to release these energies, to provide greater satisfaction in the work-place and to assist in raising the levels of productivity and efficiency in British industry-and with it the standards of living of the nation-is not by recriminations or exhortation but by putting the relationship between capital and labour on to a new basis which will involve not just management but the whole workforce in sharing responsibility for the success and profitability of the enterprises". On other assumptions, however, the central problems of management-union relations centre upon value-level considerations and above all upon the tendency for British industrial relations, in particular experience progressive normative disintegration. Such a view was eloquently put forward by fox and flanders of course a decade ago and whatever our reservations about the main thesis, on empirical counts, it would be even more easy to sustain at this juncture. Moreover, such problems of anomie in the British context are frequently contrasted with, say, experience in Western Germany in this respect as, indeed, schregle has emphasised. "Co-determination can be fully understood only if one is aware not merely of the legalistic bias in the national character but also of its reluctance to accept ongoing opposition between conflicting interests. This results in an inclination to resolve differences by integrating opposing forces into an institutional organization. Accommodation and integration, as well as order and authority, occupy an important place in the national system of values." And on two further assumptions industrial democracy may be seen as a reflection of processes of rationalisation which occasion the spread of both bureaucratic and democratic forms within the institutional framework of modern societies or an extension of the concept of citizenship into employment relations. Moreover, the first interpretation clearly reflects the Weberian understanding of the parallel growth of bureaucracy and democracy in the enterprise; while the latter is based on T.H. Marshall's interpretation of the rights of citizenship, a view recently echoed by Goldthorpe in his analysis of the sociological origins of the high rates of inflation in contemporary Britain.

Disjunctive models

In disjunctive models of industrial democracy, however, the institutions in question are viewed as merely reflections and as not necessarily as ameliorating the presumed underlying conflicts of interest between management and worker. For example, structural analysts operating from within Marxist traditions, view the emergence of participative programmes as at best fragile trues which in no measure alter the basic relationships of production at all. Thus as Ramsay has argued, "It has been suggested that a Marxist framework of analysis, based on a view of the production relations of capitalism as essentially a matter of conflict between the interests of capital and labour, provides a coherent explanation..... capitalism both engenders and renders impotent such movements foe participation". Of course, not all conflict models of industrial relations have been grounded in Marxian assumptions; and, indeed, a central postulate of, say Dahrendorf's thesis in this regard was that the most successful institutions of industrial democracy were based upon a prior recognition of the structural cleavage of interests occasioned by the distributions of authority in "imperatively co-ordinated associations". But at all events a common characteristic of all these approaches has been to examine the genesis of industrial democracy in terms of this fundamental cleavage of interests which is presumed to obtain and for the further inference to be drawn that such underlying conflicts may be best be expressed relatively peacefully via comprehensive participation programmes but remain unaltered by such changes themselves.

At times such structural-type analyses have been developed in conjunction with interpretations accommodating the perceptions of 'actors' in industrial and labour relations. But again there are a number of points of variation here although three would appear to be of special salience in this context; namely, the "rising expectations" thesis, the awareness of problems alienation at work, and the extension of wider political struggles into employment relations. Thus in a series of socio-psychological and sociological writings the rising expectations of the workforce for greater autonomy and ultimately for 'self-actualisation' has been stressed while, in similar vein, the consciousness of alienation at workplace level has also been seen as providing an insistent pressure for revitalising work roles and relationships by means of schemes not only for responsible autonomy but for participation in higher decision making committees as well. Moreover, the parallels between the political struggle for the franchise in the 19th century and the conflict over industrial democracy in the current era have been stressed; indeed, the bullock committee report again contained a trenchant passage in this regard: "Several submissions have drawn attention to the parallels between political and industrial democracy. They have argued that, just as in the 19th century the shifts in economic power to the middle and working classes made it essential to harness that power to the benefit of society, by extending the suffrage, now is the time to provide scope for the growing power and unused capacities of organize". Moreover, this fundamental distinction between integrative and disjunctive modes of participation is absolutely basic for understanding the experience of managerial personnel in the world's major experiments in industrial democracy. This is the case principally because, under integrative modes of participation, the crucial bases upon which the successful exercise of power rest especially upon expertise and knowledge and, above all, upon control over information on technical, commercial and even personnel questions. Hence, in these circumstances, the cession of extensive formal powers to democratically-elected decision making committees may account to little in practice in these respects even though it still has the vital legitimating function of producing a measure of social and even of system integration which, in turn, permits a distribution of power based upon consensual premises in the first place.

By contrast, in disjunctive modes of participation rather different bases of power are marshalled. For instance, informs based upon trade union and 'shop steward' systems, union representatives typically deploy numbers organization and various resources (e.g. skill scarcity, technical ability and, in a dispute itself, the flow of materials and labour). Meanwhile, in such situations, managements correspondingly initiate actions based upon their crucial leverage over the enterprise organizations, together with its financial resources and the right to provide or to terminate employment (with the option, in the last resort, of closing down a concern completely). The upshot, then, is a continual struggle for power in an environmental context in which wider exigencies (e.g. political and economic changes), technical movements and normative beliefs and aspirations variously favour one party or the other.

Of course, integrative modes of participation tend to sustain only those managerial personnel who fit closest to the ideal typical character of 'the managerialist' or 'managerial revolution' thesis (i.e. those who are non-propertied, technically proficient and professional); those whose authority rested previously upon ownership criteria alone are likely to be correspondingly disadvantaged. But to clarify the consequences of integrative and disjunctive types of industrial democracy for managerial personnel the following typology of outcomes along the principal dimensions of power is undoubtedly useful. Hence in the chart we have related the main power dimensions to two main integrative experiments and the familiar disjunctive model based on union-management committees.

Industrial democracy, employee participation and mangers; some empirical cases

So far out analysis of the experience of managerial personnel in ongoing and emerging experiments in industrial democracy has been primarily conceptual in its focus. In this section of our account, therefore, it is appropriate to consider the empirical and substantive issues by examining a number of key experiments in industrial democracy and employee participation. Elsewhere we have surveyed in some detail managerial experiences under co-determination and producer co-operatives and, therefore, for current purposes we have endeavoured by and large, to elaborate upon rather different instances. When taken in conjunction, however, the consistent finding over a very wide range of experiments serve to reinforce the central proposition of this chapter of the pervasive impact of managerial personnel, in practice, in the majority of instances of the phenomenon under review. Three main types of participation have thus been isolated foe verificatory purposes:-

Types of participation

(a) Managerially-sponsored experiments with

special reference to(i) joint consultation and (ii) 'commonwealth' ventures.

(b) management-union relationships at enterprise level under disjunctive bargaining.

(c) Decentralisation and self-management of enterprise.

Experiments in participation sponsored by managerial personnel

In the context of industrial democracy and employee participation, then, management strategies may be outlined by taking into account two main consideration: first, institutional and shop floor experiments initiated by managers themselves; and second, modes of group and personal adaptation to radical ventures stemming from worker, trade union, or legislative programmes. To begin with, therefore, a considerable number of human relations style.

Participation schemes based upon Zweckrational premises have been deployed by managers and these range from piecemeal attempts to raise productivity and efficiency to so-called "total involvement" exercises. In practice, a great many of these practices have amounted to little more than changes in leadership style involving no major changes in patterns of authority and control whatsoever. Indeed, most have focused upon means and short-term decisions and thereby have entailed at most a sacrifice of authority of first line levels of supervision while leaving intact top management structure (and the capacity of managerial personnel for unilateral determination of enterprise objectives) together with the existing hierarchy of control over medium and long-term decisions. Of course, at the lowest levels of supervision, substantial adaptations may have been occasioned such as in the case of Imperial Chemical Industries at its Gloucester plant, where, as Cotgrove and his colleagues demonstrated; "the adoption of a supervisory style based on participation was not easy; for some, the fundamental changes in behaviour required were more than they could manage". But for higher echelons in the management hierarchy no such radical changes in power and influence were discerned.

In terms of objectives, however, two main traditions have been dominant; the human relations emphasis upon producing harmonious shop-floor environments and the more specific managerial and employer commitment to profit and efficiency criteria. The first is reflected, for example, in the Swedish programmes for job enrichment where, as Gyllenhammar has observed, the aims were to enrich the job and to complicate things in order to enhance responsibility, increase learning possibilities, mutual respect and understanding of the total job and its relation to the world inside and outside the organization. By contrast, the second, which has particularly surfaced in conditions of enhanced trade union power, has been based upon the propositions enunciated by Walker and institutionalised in ways which typically involved no major erosion of the manager's strategic decision making control.

(1) Workers have ideas which are useful.

(2) Communications upwards are essential for accurate decision making at the top.

(3) Workers will accept decisions better if they are able to participate in them.

(4) Workers will work harder, more intelligently and more co-operatively with each other and with management if they share in decisions which affect them.

(5) Industrial democracy will contribute to industrial peace by fostering more cooperative attitudes between workers and managers and thus raise efficiency by reducing stoppages.

(6) Industrial democracy will act as a spur for managerial efficiency since management will have to think its decisions out more carefully if it has to justify them to the workers.

But the conversion of managers from a 'unitary' to a 'pluralist' view of the enterprise has been by no means universal. Indeed, as Fox has insisted, the preference for a unitary perspective rests on its utility as an ideology which serves three purposes; "It is at once a method of a self-assurance, an instrument of persuasion, and a technique of seeking legitimation of authority" The "unitary conception", too, has typically been reflected in the early inclination of managers for consultative rather than participative machinery since the former allowed merely for a measure of influence by employees over decision making while leaving control, authority and institutional power firmly in managerial hands. Hence as Clarke and his colleagues have argued "on the whole, employers and their spokesman have evinced deep mistrust as to the value of participation, particularly in integrative forms, such as the appointment of workers' directors though they reflect a widespread belief in prior consultation with workers on matters which concern them"

The joint consultative committee was thus a favoured institution of 'human relations' inspired managerial personnel committed to unitary assumptions of the proper distribution of authority in the enterprise. Indeed it was once commonplace for the distinction to be drawn between consultation and decision making, the former involving frank and open discussions within advisory committee with the latter being the prerogative of management alone. Of course, with the rise of the shop stewards' system, this distinction became increasingly blurred and many formal committees gradually fell into disuse. But the preservation of the decision making prerogatives of managerial personnel by such institutional devices still merits emphasis at this point.

Of course, there have been certain managerial personnel who have willingly sacrificed the higher points of enterprises policy and control to the workforce; yet the stubborn persistence of earlier decision making modes even in these cases has been a commonplace of empirical literature. The Scott-Bader commonwealth is thus a particularly cogent example here, for, according to Blum, it owed its existence to the 'deeply religious inspiration' of Ernest Bader, a convinced Quaker and pacifist, whose beliefs led to the formulation of entirely different concepts of the purposes of a productive enterprises than that typical of predominantly 'secular'industries. "The reduction of all products, people and nature itself to marketable objects; capital accounting rather than merely marketing accounting became dominant and the principles of sound finance ruled over all human considerations; the transformation of all flesh, mind, heart and soul into prices and costs; the subordination of one group under another group thus making people means for the purposes of other people; the neglect of the ethics of inrerpersonal relationships and hence the separation of people from each other and from any humanly meaningful purpose-rule of impersonal market forces over all and of personal authority over most people; finally a division of labour without balance and consideration of human values". Against such a backcloth and to avoid the problem of 'participation in the administration of evil', Bader thus sought to establish a different order in which patterns of ownership and control were both substantially modified. The commonwealth thus incorporated common ownership, the development of new channels of participation, the divestment of the right to dispose of profit, the gradual transference of power to members of the commonwealth and a division of power into legislative, executive and judicial organs. Again, the main legislative body was the general meeting and all members of the commonwealth could participate in administrative and judicial areas as well.

Nevertheless, notwithstanding the provisions in the constitution for direct participation by employees and the many further opportunities to participate-especially in departmental meetings-it was clear that 'people with managerial responsibility or people from the laboratory participated more actively than factory and maintenance people'. And this was particularly important in the light of the fact that, as with most integrative modes of participation, the greater security enjoyed by members of the commonwealth, by comparison with their colleagues in industry at large, militated against unionisation.

Management-union relationships at enterprises level under disjunctive bargaining

Nonetheless in the bulk of managerially-initiated programmes for participation there have been a series of device built into the schemes themselves in order to avoid a wholesale transference of the manager's decision making power to the ordinary worker. Moreover, as we have just observed, even in the empirically rare instances of a major divestment of control and authority to the workforce, in practice, effectiveness in participation, the capacity to influence decisions and to ensure a substantial measure of de facto rather than de jure power over policy still largely resides in managerial hands. Of course, the objection would be reasonably raised that managerial-initiated programmes offer at best a partial guide to the experience of managerial personnel under participative governance more generally and hence it is with a view of surveying a number of radically different ventures that our attention now appropriately turns.

There can be no major doubt, then, that in countries such as Great Britain, the predominant modes of participation have been of a disjunctive character, since they have been based primarily upon the workplace union organization and shop stewards' systems. Moreover, under such arrangements diverse or plural centres of authority are recognised although control, formally at least, and with it ultimate responsibility for the affairs of the establishment, resides under the juristiction of the salaried managerial personnel of the concern in question.

But if under disjunctive participation, managerial control is undisturbed, there is clearly a major check upon power and influence and upon the functioning of companies themselves. Hence, as Batstone and his colleagues have remarked; "shop stewards have often been seen as a major cause of wage inflation, disruptions to production, and other checks upon profitable company operation.... There can be little doubt that the shop-floor domestic organization had a very important impact upon production management..... In brief, the power of the domestic organization meant that management had little freedom in introducing any form change in production which might have an adverse impact upon workers.

Major changes in production methods involved possibly lengthy negotiations over effort and reward. The same was true of short-term changes. If management required temporary variations or exceptional patterns of work, they were generally bound either by negotiations or by a network of rules which were the product of past negotiation". To be sure, beyond the production area, the stewards' attempts to influence management's behaviour proved to be remarkably limited. For example, accounting procedures, investment decisions, marketing, pricing and purchasing policies tended to remain almost exclusively 'managerial prerogatives'. Moreover, these data reaffirm the earlier attempts to map out the range and scope of issues with which shop stewards are concerned at workplace level. Hence, as will be recalled, the work of the Royal Commission on trade unions and employers' associations included an assessment of the stewards' range of bargaining in British industry and revealed that while nearly three-quarters of the sample discussed and settled working conditions as a standard practice, the proportion was reduced to just over one-half for wages questions and even less for discussions on hours of work, discipline and employment issues. However, in a further investigation it was disclosed that 70 per cent of managements included in the sample were not free to organize the workforce as they wished and that the principal areas controlled by the shop floor included labour mobility, manning of machines, job demarcation, hampering work study, resistance to dilutees and union demarcation.

In short, then, managerial control over the bulk of strategic decisions remains intact under disjunctive bargaining, although authority, power and influence over a number of issues are more evenly shared. Similarly, at shop floor level in particular, managerial freedom for innovation and manoeuvre are in many cases extremely circumscribed. But it remains of interest that the four-fold increase in number of full-time shop stewards in British industry in the course of the 1970's and their widespread expansion of influence over decision making processes were themselves very much stimulated by managerial actions.

Managerial personnel and the ventures in self-management

But what happens to the manager in radical, integrative ventures in self-management in which, in terms of initiative, broader political agencies have been the dominant agency? For our final example we turn appropriately to the experience of workers' councils and self-management of enterprises paying special attention of course, to the Yugoslavian case. In this experience it will be demonstrated that although formal control over policy resides in the workforce, in practice, influence and power in particular are exercised predominantly by managerial personnel.

The details of the statutory framework of the Yugoslavian enterprise are too familiar to merit lengthy treatment, but as will be recalled, the principal organs consist of the worker's council, management board and director. And above all, of course, in each workplace, a worker's council, elected by the entire labour force, is given overall responsibility for policy and entrusted with the legal obligation to determine general economic activity of the works. But if we turn to examine the roles in practice, two general conclusions may be drawn; that the influence of workers on decision-making processes is restricted by comparison with that exercised by higher managerial personnel, and that it has declined progressively in the absence of external administrative pressures. The evidence from studies deploying the control-graph method, too, tends to support the claim that administrative staff 'have power without responsibility' and 'the council responsibility without power'.

Supplementary material from observational studies of workers' councils in practice tends to corroborate these findings. Kolaja, in both the factories he investigated, discovered that managers were able to ensure that all the measures in which they were interested were implemented by the workers' council, that those suggestions which were adopted by the council derived, in the majority of cases from the managers, and that only the better educated workers were effective in discussions. And certainly the view that managers lose all their effective decision making powers under workers' councils systems was to prove utterly groundless.

Again, in a further survey, Bertsch and Obradovic have shown that workers clearly have less influence than managers in the self-management system despite the widespread advocacy by the latter of the desirability of an increase in non-managerial power. But, while other sectors were not excluded, technical and managerial staffs have been found to be ascendant in council meetings; data which reinforce the earlier conclusion by obradovic that "deliberations in these councils are largely dominated by high-level managers and technical experts.... with the result that the rank-and-file members participate less actively than theory might suggest".

Yet none of the foregoing suggests that, from a worker's point of view substantial benefits have not accrued from self-management systems.

On the contrary, as the IDE researchers have demonstrated, outside power sources can be important in given politico-economic contexts, while Yugoslavia appears to be the one exception to the so-called "hierarchical two-peaked" pattern of influence (i.e. the occurrence of a sharp peak for top management followed by a slump at the next level and another smaller peak for representative bodies). Hence, while in Yugoslavia, formal rules regulating intraorganizational decision making have been clearly shown to favour top managers; equally, the representative peaked pattern was found to be unique to that country. Similarly, taking organizations in the European countries covered in the study in question as a whole, it was only in Yugoslavia that centralised, closed, non-democratic and management centred decision making structures were not predominant and this was despite the fact that "formal rules might be seen as promoting an inverse hierarchical ordering since formal power rests much more with representative bodies than with top management.

Indeed in socialist countries in particular, managerial personnel would appear to be the principal beneticiaries of any "withering away of the state" and of the consequent diminution in the powers of external administrative agencies to control the affairs of the enterprise. Hence, the decentralist initiatives which have typically accompanied the spawning of workers' council and self-management systems in the first instance have further produced a non zero sum situation insofar as the members of industrial concerns are concerned and resulted, pari passu, in an expansion of workers' control alongside an augmentation of managerial power and influence particularly over commercial and technical questions.

7 Technology, Work Structure, and Group Behaviour

Technology, work, structure, and group behavior

This study was designed to explore a very elementary unit in the structure of industrial relations, the work group. It focused on the behavior of work groups and particularly on concerted behavior actuated by the self-interests of the members. Our objectives was to explain differences in behavior among work groups. We wished to discover whether certain aspects of employee day-to-day behavior could be related to the *structure of the work group*, as determined by the technology of the enterprise, independent of supervisory skills, management and union pressures and individual personality variables.

At the level of everyday observation we find that each plant has certain departments that are more troublesome or more cooperative than the average. The incidence of serious breaches of plant discipline such as wildcat strikes and the occurrence of formal and informal grievances are not randomly distributed. Some related studies have shown that participation in intraunion activities is also concentrated in a relatively small proportion of the total plant population. Both managers and union officers often take into account the existence and the influence of these informal clusters of workers.

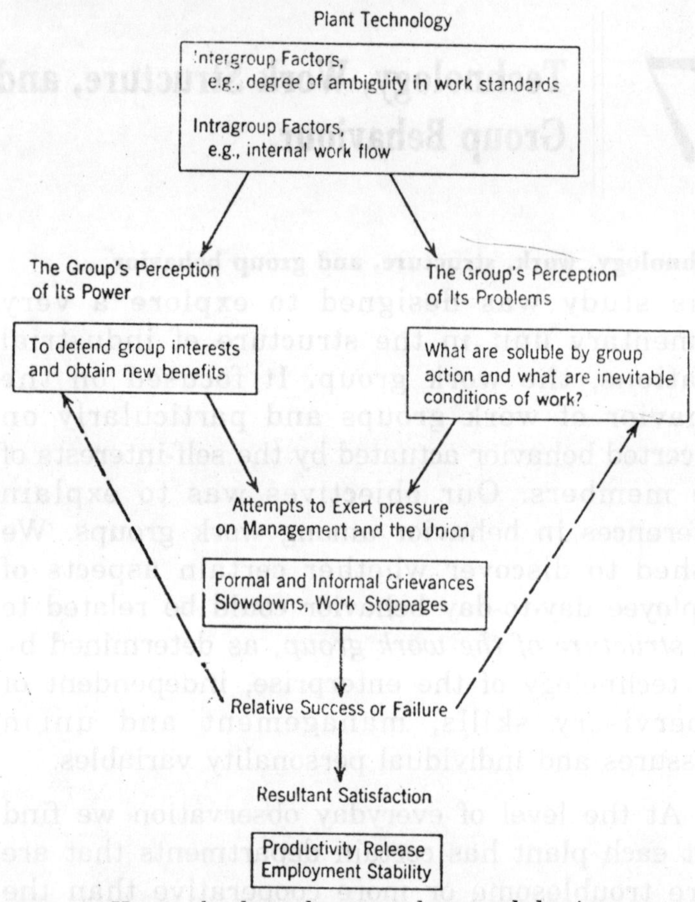

How technology shapes work group behavior

Our basic theme has been: although at any one time particular work groups may tend to be more management or union oriented, such attitudes are less important in explaining the industrial relations life of the plant, than the *dynamic relationships among concerted interest aggregations.* At a particular period some of these groups may be in relative equilibrium, but many are motivated to gain new benefits or defend old ones. Their efforts in such endeavors will be instrumental in shaping the effectiveness of management and union policies.

The above illustrates diagrammatically the relation of plant technology to work group behavior. Technology directly affects the group's perceptions of both the work problems it believes are soluble by concerted effort and the relative power it can muster to do battle for these. In turn, these two factors are responsible for the number and quality of pressure tactics utilized against management and the union. The success or failure of these efforts to originate changes in benefits enjoyed contributes to employment stability and productivity. These experiences also feed back information shaping group judgment on whether future forays for similar objectives are worth future sacrifices.

We also hoped to add in some small measure to the understanding of plant-level industrial relations. We believe that a relatively small number of work groups within an industrial relations character. The behavior of the groups and its sources are, we believe,, predictable. Further, the total manufacturing process sets very real limits to the effectiveness of certain patterns of supervision and union-management relationships.

To many it may have appeared naive, even misleading, to discuss grievance behavior, as often as we have, without more explicit reference to the nature of the issues involved, and the positions of the parties to the dispute. Surely, it will be argued, grievances, slow-downs strikes, all must be related to what employees, managers, and union leaders struggle over within the plant. This fact can hardly be denied. But what was appeared of equal significance is that the *quantity* of dissatisfaction expressed and its *quality* were relatable to specific organizational variables. What one group saw as a problem another group might be willing to accept as an inevitable conditions of work. The attitudes of employees were a product of the structural conditions of work.

This type of analysis has also involved a concept of the grievance procedure in industry which is broader than the rather legalistic definitions incorporated in union-management contacts. Employee protests, complaints, grievances, and pressure tactics, are all efforts to communicate upward in the organization, to initiate change. This is in. contrast to the more usual position they fill in the organization: responding to the orders and initiations of both management and union representatives. In such a process it is impossible to separate the true grievances from the efforts at negotiating more advantageous conditions of work, or from aggressive demonstrations of accumulated frustrations.

That we can predict which *departments* or work groups in a particular plant will exhibit these kinds of behavior, without knowing the specific composition of the group, the qualities of the supervisor, or the state of union-management relations. We can, in fact, make such judgments with a fair degree of accuracy. In a given plant certain work groups will consistently exhibit characteristic behavior even though their supervisor is changed and union-management relations mature or deteriorate. We very often find that certain occupational groups are known throughout an industry for their highly characteristic behavior. These similarities of behavior, associated with a given kind or type of work group, are the subject of our research.

Significance of occupation

At one level, this is a study of the significances of occupation, of type of work, for the demonstrated behavior of job incumbents. Although the study concentrates on a relatively narrow group of "blue-collar" jobs, it is hoped that some of the same techniques, and some of the same variables as well will be applicable to a much wider range of occupations.

A substantial amount of research in the social science has indicated that the worker is occupationally oriented, men are bound together by shared work experiences and attitudes. We usually think of "occupation" as referring to the well-defined professions and crafts as well as the "would be" professions and trades. Employees in the modern factory, with its emphasis on machine output, with the exception of a small number of traditional craftsmen required to occupational pattern, except the very broad one of "semiskilled factory worker". Except for membership in this amorphous classification, industrial workers are not thought to have other occupational ties. A close examination of the day-to-day functioning of the plant, however, belies this assumption. Sought to explore the basis for this identification and its impact on the plant and more particularly the kinds of differences that develop among plant occupations.

Significance of technology

More specifically, this report should have some significance for the industrial engineer, the student of organization and work flow, and the manager who is concerned with the relationship between the manufacturing process and human relations. In another context the author has expressed his view that engineering variables and personnel variables are not unrelated, and that the "human relations approach" involves an understanding of the relation of technology to the functioning of the organization.

Ideally, it should be possible to develop predictive tools that would permit the design of organizations for specific personnel or industrial relations characteristics. The millennium is nowhere in sight, we quickly add, but our research should move us ion this direction. A society characterized by a dynamic technology can ill afford to ignore the relation of this technology to the reactions of the work force recruited to man the machines and factories plans, job classification, seniority and all the rest, and most specifically to the grievance procedure.

Both management and the union reserve such epithets as "prima donnas", "troublemakers," and "hot heads" for groups whose motives and behavior in the plant community leave something to be desired. Although they prefer to believe radical leadership is the cause, this hypothesis is quickly destroyed. We have seen, for example, strategic or Erratic behavior patterns are perpetuated over long periods, although the offending leaders may have been removed, and the objects of the aggression eliminated.

However, we did observe certain groups which were more susceptible to the personalities of strong leaders. We concluded that Apathetic and Erratic groups sought out and responded positively to charismatic leaders. Thus, if they were subject to the influence of a highly aggressive individual, with the ability to attract a following, they might develop more hostile relations with management; or the union than if no such member was included within their group. At the same time they were also subject to rapid conversions to good relations through some newly acquired leader.

We also sought to explain overall differences among the industrial relations climates of some of the plants in the study. Plants where most operations were technologically interdependent were likely to be highly cooperative or highly antagonistic in their union-management relations. Those with a number of insulated, self-sufficient departments could not easily fall into either of these extreme relationships, because the union officers were kept occupied responding to the insistent self-interest demands of these work groups. Relations in these plants were in the middle range, neither outstandingly good nor bad.

What is human relations research?

One further value of this kind of research ɿay be to highlight some misconceptions concerning the nature of human relations research. Many critics see the developing field of human relations as emphasizing solely interpersonal *communications* variables. The typical problem they believe is dealt with here is lack of common understanding due to individual ineptness, or personality difficulties. The critics believe the findings of human relations research could be summarized as follows: "If you can somehow cause people to 'see the other fellow's point of view,' any conflict of interest between them will disappear". The causal factors, these critics feel, are always personal, individual shortcomings.

Given this consumption, perhaps overstated, it is no wonder that observers who recognize the influence of environmental and historical forces in human relations are hostile or, at best, amused at the naivete that would place such heavy weight on face-to-face relations or group dynamics.

In fact, many researchers who are blanketed-in under the reproachful term "human relations" deal directly and specifically with environmental forces, particularly structural forces. One conclusion of the present study is that broad technological factors play a significant role in determining the characteristics of work group behavior.

To be sure, some researchers, as well as management, have tended to put human relations and problems relating to the organization of work in separate, watertight compartments. Under these assumptions the researcher is either interested in the skills of dealing with the human element at work or the engineering problem of efficient organizational design. Although it is possible to change the pattern of human relations in the organization without changing the technology, the arrangement of jobs, and the organizational structure, the reverse is probably not true.

Informal groups as a means of participation

On the subject of worker participation in plant decisions affecting their livelihood and satisfactions, we tend to restrict our thinking to two rather distinct levels. On the one hand, we have the development of research and practice on methods by which the supervisor can effectively utilize the subordinate groups to complement his own leadership and decision-making ability. This has the advantages of more economical use of employees ideas and knowledge, and greater likelihood that worker support will be given to decisions finally made. On the other hand, the literature of union-management relations stresses the role of unions in giving the worker an opportunity to participate in industrial management.

Successful in influencing both the decisions of their supervisors and the policies and programs of their local unions when they act in concert-through the medium of their own work groups. It is at this intermediate level, perhaps more than at any other, that worker points of view and interests can be effective in influencing the thinking of the union leadership and the company management. The local union is an organization which cannot automatically serve the multifarious and often conflicting needs of members who owe allegiance to it. Few political organizations, in fact, will be responsive to a rabble of individuals.

Insofar as common interests are represented in the informal group, their expression will be amplified many times beyond the single voice in the department meeting or individual grievance in the union files.

On a more theoretical level there is no reason why we should distinguish between the interactions involved in the more traditional superior-subordinate decision-making process and those relevant to the redress procedures embodied in the collective bargaining agreement. In terms of the social system of the factory, there is no difference. Both can involve participation, or upward initiation, as we would define the concept.

Management is often told that it must learn to work with "groups" since employees, under many circumstances, do not respond as individuals to company action. In fact, it is becoming almost commonplace to speak of the supervisor's responsibility for learning to deal effectively with his subordinates as an informal group, with its unique leadership, beliefs, and customs. Research in recent years has given rise to a whole new conception of leadership that involves the utilization of group methods: conferences, group decision, and representative shop government.

In all of the discussions of working with the informal group, there is a tacit assumptions that basically all groups are alike, and the only unique feature with which the supervisor need acquaint himself is the fact that a group is something other than the sum of the individuals included, that there is a plus factor which makes the whole something more than the sum of its parts. A good deal of effort therefore goes into teaching supervisors what a group "is."

In a sense, in this report we are challenging the previous assertion. We are suggesting that there are highly significant differences among work groups, and before the supervisor can deal effectively with the work group, he needs to know much more about these differences. Often we have tended mistakenly to place full responsibility on the supervisor for his group's behavior: Employee-centered supervisors are supposed to build prideful work groups that are likely to demonstrate high productivity. While the supervisor's behavior is certainly not without effect, our data would indicate that there are many facets of group behavior which can more readily be related to the internal structure of the group and its relative position in the total plant structure than to the behavior of the supervisor. Hence, a work group is not one pattern of employee responses, but rather a whole range of possible behavior.

We have suggested that to explain this range of group behavior we need to relate the work structure and the associated social structure to their potential foe economic interest groupings. Realistically, we can no longer ignore the fact that workers in unionized plants attempt to protect and improve what they feel is important about their jobs through group action, and these groups cannot be separated from work and social aggregations. The complexity of our discussion has been primarily due to this attempt to explain the dynamic relation between work teams, friendship cliques, and pressure groups. We have attempted to suggest possible interrelations between these kinds of groups, the power they exert, the satisfaction they provide their members, and the level of productivity they motivate.

Thus, the informal work group is something more than an unplanned-for modification of the formal organization that influences workers' attitudes and ties them together in meaningful social wholes. It is also a dynamic factor in shaping the critical pressures and decisions which are partially responsible for the industrial relations climate of the plant. In some instances these interest groupings can move the plant toward disequilibrium rather than toward the snug harmony and balance envisioned by Mayo and his followers.

8 Control, Choice and Purpose in Industrial Relations

In the first section of this volume we were primarily concerned with delineating patterns of stability and change in the organizational and occupational roles of managers and with outlining the significance of the relationship between corporate control and professional aspiration. This, in turn, formed a backloth against which the foregoing analysis of managerial strategies could be developed in the context of three issues of special relevance for modern industrial relations theory and practice: social responsibility, payment systems and industrial democracy. In the final part of this study, therefore, the question of managerial objectives in industrial relations will be further evaluated by focusing not only upon the conventionally interpreted functions of the labour or personnel specialist but also the individual and group responses of managers to modifications in their occupational roles and in their relative esteem and remuneration vis-a-vis other members of the enterprise.

The objectives of this chapter are thus twofold. First, we shall highlight, if only rather briefly, a number of central themes in the literature on the development and change of the managerial industrial relations function; and second, our account will form a prelude to the three subsequent reviews of the ways in which a series of economic, political and social changes have occasioned a coterminous expansion of professional associations and managerial trade unionism. Yet, as we shall also indicate, there are considerable dangers in adopting too short a time scale for the analysis. After all, there have been a series of industrial relations forays over the last two decades which, despite optimistic and often worthy intentions of their advocates, have clearly not ushered in any 'new dawn' in employer-employee relations. Indeed, this state of affairs has been manifest recently by the attempts by managers, in a variety of industrial and service enterprises, to reassert executive as well as corporate control over decision making processes.

The discussions which follow, therefore, will be developed in a manner which is designed deliberately to highlight a number of central themes in the discipline of industrial relations. To this end, our account will commence by examining the crucial questions of "control" versus "choice" insofar as managements' actions in industrial relations are concerned. Second, we shall argue, perhaps controversially, that for much of the current century, the manager's role has been highly active in the labour and personnel fields and that the evidence is far from consistent with the commonly held but unfounded thesis of passivity in the face of dominant initiatives by trade unions and the state. Third, we shall endeavour to map out a number of "causative" influences upon the shape and growth of personnel and labour relations departments, which are conceived of here as crucial components of the management *organization* of industrial relations. Fourth, the currently fashionable "human resources" question will be addressed as part of a brief examination of future prospects. And lastly, we shall seek to shift the basic paradigm in which conventional analyses have been conducted by reviewing the theme of managers *in* industrial relations. That is to say, we shall depict mangers, not only as the occupants of superordinate roles within the enterprise, but also as a special group of employees, possessing a distinctive conception of their own interests, which, increasingly, they have sought to prosecute through the policies and programmes of a variety of managerial association.

"Control", "Choice" and the primary focus of the industrial relations of managers

Insofar as debates on the central premises of the discipline of industrial relations are concerned, undoubtedly the most significant have been between the so-called "rules" versus "control" schools. Of course, as we have argued at a number of points in this volume, both approaches are in one sense narrow in compass since the notions of choice between different strategies and objectives and the associated concepts of creativity and freedom are treated unsatisfactorily in the respective formulations. At the same time, however, in adapted from, both remain important milestones in the conceptual advance of the discipline and hence, although a detailed review of the principal arguments would be superfluous here, equally, it is essential at the outset to highlight the principal implications of these perspectives outset to highlight the principal implications of these perspectives for the general theme of the modern manager and industrial relations.

It will be familiar, then, that the original conception of industrial relations outlined by Dunlop and Flanders entailed a primacy of emphasis upon the genesis and application of rules within systems. To be sure , there remained important differences in this respect, since Dunlop, in particular, had sought to steer the discipline away from what he understood to be the narrow confines of British analysis upon the institutions of collective bargaining, revealing a preference instead for a focus upon the much wider ensemble of rule-making processes which could evolve in systems which were bereft of any recognisable independent associations of working people whatsoever, Yet, in the 1970's, the premises of both these approaches were subjected to major challenges; most noticeably from those scholars who regarded the question of control over decision making processes as ultimately crucial for industrial relations. Of course, the points of difference between these conception have often been overstated of difference between these conceptions have often been overstated not least because regulation, especially, is normally defined in terms of *control by rule*. But in our view, both approaches are currently in need of further revision, partly in order to countenance the increasingly widespread empirical evidence of the saliency of social action and cultural variables, but also to accommodate the way in which the *choice* of internal organizational structure at enterprise level can substantially inform the objectives and day to day operation of specific industrial relations systems.

More explicitly, therefor, recent theoretical and empirical advances would appear to suggest that to emphasise rules or control without prior recognition of the dimensions of choice, creativity and freedom is inadmissible in any contemporary definition of the primary points of focus in the study of industrial relations. After all, not only are the ultimate purposes of rules or control absolutely crucial here but also models based upon structural, organizational or institutional *determinism* ar ultimately of even greater significance the *acquiescence* of the bulk of the participant actors. The consequential abrogation of responsibility for action may indeed be associated with what Sahay has termed "the profound misunderstanding of the modern age... that freedom can be given to people". After all, not only is it always theirs if they want it, but those claiming to champion the freedom of others are enabled so to do only because of "the corruption of the will to freedom" which in turn seems to have bee born out "of the fear of the individual against the powers that be, thus, quite logically, making the legitimation of the existing structures of power and authority possible through acquiescence". In short, the conception of structural or organizational determinism arises precisely in those eras in which an abrogation of choice by the bulk of the populace has been widely institutionalised.

Nonetheless, the significance of "voluntarism" within certain manifest constraints would seem to be an increasingly common finding of empirically-based as well as general surveys. For example, in a recent study analysing the variations in worker participation in different European counties, it has been demonstrated how choice played an important part in the establishment of formal rules, influence and involvement, its significance being no less marked in the case of managerial practice in industrial relations. "Our study suggests that high levels of employee participation are a function of an intricate interrelation of internal managerial practices and externally promoted support systems based on formal laws or collective bargaining agreements.

Further, both these variables together do a better job of predicting influence and power distribution than "objective" technological or structural conditions such as organizational size, internal differentiation, or levels of automation. This last finding underscores the "voluntaristic" nature of industrial democracy in the underscores a system which is more the outcome of socio-political factors than of structural opportunities or constraints."

Again, as Anthony has insisted, although managements cannot ensure the fulfilment of all their objectives unless they enjoy "sufficient power to be able to exercise coercive, unilateral control over the workforce"; equally, in circumstances when they are able to enforce decisions "upon passive or acquiescent employees... their affairs do not belong in a study of industrial relations". And by he same token, of course, certain forms of workers' or union control would likewise eliminate the very possibility of a discipline of industrial relations.

A properly formulated notion of choice must, therefore, in our view, be central to the study of industrial relations; a position which, ironically, was once well understood in certain management science circles. Indeed, as Thomason has observed, the major tensions in the enterprise can be identified by setting "in the form of a matrix, the answer to the question for whose benefit? the activity is undertaken against the level of decision involved, corporate administrative". In short, on such formulations, control properly occupies a derivative position in the overall priorities of the enterprise, with policy, strategy, method and interest all being, in the last analysis, far more fundamental premises of action.

But, once control is regarded as ultimately facilitative rather than as the sole objective of industrial relations institutions and actors' behaviour, it is then possible to deploy the notion in an analytically fruitful fashion. Certainly, as we observed in the chapter on industrial democracy, and as David Simpson argues in the ensuing account, it constitutes a valuable reference point for understanding the dilemmas of modern managerial personnel in industrial relations. Again Weber and Dahrendorf had earlier observed that the structural division of roles into positions of formal control and authority and the separation of skill s from the materials of work in bureaucratic organizations constitute indisputable sources of friction. Moreover, echoing these concerns, Anthony has referred to the inevitability of managers seeking control, while Smith has insisted that the mission of the labour movement is to extend the frontier of control; departures which, in practice, are liable to produce latent or manifest forms of industrial conflict.

By the same token, there is little doubt that the 'control thesis' has a number of advantages over the traditional collective bargaining approach. Indeed, as Smith has rightly observed, there are at least three important deficiencies of the latter perspective: (a) the narrowness of its compass and its exclusion of many factors outside institutions which regulate employer-employee relations; (b) its inapplicability in many industrial relations systems in countries with no collective bargaining machinery and where regulation takes the form of law, social custom and convention or compulsory arbitration; and (c) the neglect of management's role in industrial relations with the result that attention is directed away "from corporate head offices towards manufacturing plants which appear to be the centre of action; and away from decision-making in policy terms towards the techniques of negotiation and the conflict situations surrounding those techniques."

Management and industrial relations: initiatives and constraints

In much of the industrial relations literature over the last decade or so the manger, therefore, has not only been the true ghost at the bargaining table, but the formulation of his objectives and strategies in industrial relations has remained largely uncharted. On one view, this dearth in knowledge stems from the logical application of the assumption that the trade unions and the state and the legislature have been the primary forces shaping modern patterns of industrial relations. Yet if we turn our attention to the question of the manager' role in industrial relations by focusing, in the first instance, upon objectives and constraints, the blatant fallacies of such a premise will be readily appreciated.

For much of the 1960's and 1970's the industrial relations function was the principal growth point of business administration. Indeed, the rapid expansion of personnel and industrial relations departments, the increasing involvement in policy and strategy, and even the re-emergence of employees' associations after a period of dormancy were all symptomatic of a rapidly expanding commitment in managerial and employer circles to industrial relations questions.

Again, although the report itself is now largely only on historical interest, the Royal Commission on Trade Unions and Employers' Associations had earlier set its seal of approval on the growth of managerial involvement in the personnel and industrial relations sphere; as, indeed, Brown has recorded: "A basic distinction was drawn between the `formal' system of industry-wide collective bargaining embodied in official institutions and the `informal system' of bargaining over piece-work, additions to basic wage rates, and overtime bargaining embodied in official institutions and the `informal system' of bargaining over piece-work, additions to basic wage rates, and overtime earnings at factory level, which were seen as largely out of the control of employers and their association and of unions... The solutions to the problems these posed was seen to lie in managerial initiatives to the problems these posed was seen to lie in managerial initiatives at company and/or factory level, in cooperation with the unions, to establish orderly and effective collective bargaining procedures and to re-establish agreed control over pay and working practices." By the same token, to a considerable extent, the quadrupling in the number of full-time shop stewards in the last ten years or so would appear to have been attributable to managerial attempts to fashion systematic processes of domestic bargaining following on from the overall strategy advocated by the Royal Commission itself. Hence, as Hyman has argued, "if Donovan today seems `strangely out-of-date', this is in part because of the very success of the managerial strategy which the Report encouraged and articulated."

Yet although, doubtless, a number of structural exigencies and changing patterns in the distribution of power have operated as a constraint on strategies, the extent of managerial involvement in industrial relation may be readily appreciated by reference to the abrupt shifts in policy and objectives over the recent period. Moreover, the significance of such radical departures underscores yet again the saliency of subjective variables and of social choice in these key respects. Indeed, adopting the pattern outlined by Purcell and Smith , it would seem possible to delineate the following sequence of managerial forays in industrial relations, certain of which were founded, in the first instance, almost entirely upon active management initiatives.

(a) *Incentive payment schemes*: allowing management, workers and unions to meet "their objectives of profitability, motivation, high pay and an element of self-determination".

(b) *Productivity bargaining:* supported by governments and favored "as a means of increasing management control and broadening the scope of collective bargaining."

(c) *Plant or company bargaining*: given a further impetus from Donovan and justified as a means of "satisfying and institutionalising workplace demands, giving local management more flexibility to manage within their establishment and recognizing the potential role of joint shop stewards' committees as appropriate channels for the representation of workers' interests."

(d) *Industrial democracy and participation*; encouraged by the debates around the Bullock Report but as yet not institutionalised. From a management's point of view the advantages were seen as integrative, form the union's they were in terms of the extension of control as a major step forward in self-determination."

(e) *Recent attempts to deal more directly with the workforce and, if necessary by-passing the shop-stewards' as well as the official union machinery*. A relation of managerial objectives in a period of high inflation and intensive international competition coupled with a diminution in the power of labour as a result of high unemployment.

Of course, such strategies were formulated in differing environmental, organizational and institutional milieux and there are equally a number of obvious constraints or "controls" on managerial behaviour. Indeed, as Flanders once observed, there are four classes of social control which can impinge on managerial action; market , countervailing power, the rule of law and accountability. But such controls can engender a wide range of options from accommodation to manipulation to participation. Moreover, even if the union-orientated manager may be expected to favour the kind of strategy outlined by Purcell, a considerable measure of activity on the part of managerial personnel would be required to bring such premises of action to fruition. Hence, in Purcell's view, a management strategy for industrial relations should encompass the encouragement of union membership and the closed shop; support for membership participation in unions; the facilitation of inter-union cooperation; the institutionalisation of irreducible conflict; the maximisation of areas of avoidable conflict; the maximisation of areas of common intrests, the reduction of power of strategic groups; and the development of effective control systems . Yet, in reality, this constitutes only one of series of possible "blueprints; which particular managers may articulate in radically different ways in disparate enterprise contexts.

The managerial organization of industrial relations: The traditional paradigm

But managerial activity in industrial relations over the last decade or so has been reflected not only in the formulation and implementation of strategic policies and objectives but also in the attention paid to establishing specialist organizations at workplace and corporate levels. This after departure has been reflected not least in the rapid expansion in the number of personnel officers in British industry as well as in private and public services. Indeed, Clegg thousand personnel specialists employed in these various sectors in the united Kingdom. Similarly, although as we shall observe later, the status of personnel managers has been a perennial source of concern, it would appear that their salaries are increasingly commenstrate with those of other members of the management team, while access to the boardroom would appear to be more open than was once the case.

At this juncture, therefore, our attention will focus upon the growth of personnel departments as crucial elements in the managerial organization of industrial relations. After considering a number of general factors associated with this expansion we shall examine variations in policy and identify the diverse objective of personnel specialists themselves. This, in turn, will form the basis for a review of the parallel development of employers' associations in the recent past.

It should be emphasised to being with, however, that the role of personnel or of "human resourcing" in the enterprise has always been ambiguous, since, throughout history, managers in general have almost invariably accepted some ultimate responsibility for industrial relations. Indeed, even today a considerable volume of "personnel business" is handled not by staff specialists but by members of the line hierarchy. Moreover, as Watson has observed: "The personnel management task has to be carried out in any organization which employs human beings as resources. And as such organizations have increased in size and as the resource of labour has, for a variety of reasons, become an increasingly significant source of uncertainty for the controllers of organizations, so we have seen an increasing number of specialists engaged in various aspects of the personnel management task. The twentieth century has seen the steady emergence of a recognisable occupation: an increasingly self-aware group of people undertaking work careers which involve full-time attention to the labour resources of advanced industrial capitalist society.'

In the present century, then, we have seen both a general increase in management's attention to "human resource" questions, since any person in a managerial or supervisory function cannot escape the "management of personnel", and also the escalating tendency for industrial relations to evolve into a functional specialism within an overall corporate conception of enterprise policy, administration and execution of objectives. And although this is not the place, of course, to enter into any lengthy discourse on the origins of such a phenomenon, it is worth sketching number of general tendencies which are of relevance to out central themes.

The growth in the attention paid to personnel and industrial relations problems and, above all, their codification in specialist departments *within* the management function has typically been understood as a response to historical changes arising out of industrialisation and modernisation. Moreover, such forces have been seen as occasioning major problems of social and system integration bringing in their train the fundamental issue of the utilization of working people as human resources. Again, in functionalist terms, the rise of personnel specialists may be envisaged as the outcome of an attempt to secure a measure of accommodation and upheavals and from the long-run force of the "spirit of rationalization". Similarly as Thomason has observed: "The origins of what is now called personnel management lie in the developments in industry during the three decades around the turn of the century. this was a period in which, in Britain, industrial reationalization involving significant increases in scale and in the division of labour first made itself felt."

Moreover, as the same author has argued, these organizational changes ushered in by employers and managers resulted in the formation of larger 'aggregates of labour' and entailed not only the further separation of functions between employers and employee but also a changing focus of loyalties on the part of the latter. Again, this situation in turn demanded managerial action in order to reassert a measure of overall enterprise control and to re-establish responsibility for the direction of corporate policy and administration. by the same token, too with an increasingly precise designation of organizational and occupational roles, employment and training became more sophisticated, producing the twin rationales of "paternalism" and "efficiency" which still manifest themselves in the personnel responsibilities of contemporary managers.

yet within these broad historical movements there have been considerable fluctuations in emphasis upon personnel and industrial relations problems in the enterprise and in the degree to which these have evolved as specialist managerial functions. Moreover, to explain these variations, as was noted in Chapter 5, a range of 'structural' 'subjective' and 'power' variables may well be relevant. In brief, then, the development of personnel work in the enterprise would seem to reflect oscillations in the following central forces:

1. *Structural changes*: Technology, enterprise size and concentration, organizational factor and the financial viability of the enterprise.

2. *Managerial values*: Social choice and initiative, the scientific management movement, human relations philosophies; socio-psychological and behavioural science experiments.

3. *Changes in power in industry and society*: The growth of trade unions and domestic bargaining, governmental and legislative interventions.

In general, therefore, the conditions which favour the growth of managerial commitment to industrial relations include: a rapid pace of technological change, growing size of enterprise, independent initiatives informed by "human relations" and other social science findings, high union power and legislative penetration. And, by way of contrast, the small-scale enterprise expriencing only limited technical and organizational change with a management committed to production rather than welfare objectives, an absence of trade unions, and only limited state participation in the industrial relations field have genrally been conditions unfavoruable to th separating out of a viable specialist personnel management function.

Nevertheless, the status and objectives of personal specialists within the managerial hierarchy have been bay no means unambiguous. On the contrary, whilst it may be the case, as Watson has insisted, that resources in achieving the successful meeting of goals set or defined by the dominant coalition"; equally, as the same author has indicated: "The members of personnel departments are forced to pay attention to both the formally rational criteria of productivity, profit, effectiveness and the rest as well as the human needs, interests and aspirations of employees which, if not attended to, may lead to the formally rational means subverting the substantially rationally conceived ends of the ultimate controllers of organizations."

This considerable ambivalence in the functions of personnel departments is thus compounded by problems of status and authority of the members themselves within the overall management structure. In a range of disparate enquiries, then, the difficulties which beset personnel in sales, production and financial departments has been a common finding. Naturally, personnel officers have sought to end what Thomason has termed a "trash can/maid -of- all- work" image, but this in no way invalidates the proposition that a low status in the managerial structure can have major consequences for the principal operation of the personnel department in industrial relations affairs. Certainly as we have elsewhere demonstrated, if the personnel department have insufficient authority to deal with labour and industrial relations questions it tends to be avoided by both line managers and *powerful* shop stewards at least insofar as the resolution and containment of disputes are concerned.

Yet if only to underscore the saliency of choice in this regard, it is also clear that personnel specialists have variously adapted to role strain and to their different source of occupational loyalty. To be sure, as Watson has pointed out, most officers would appear to seek and organizational rather than an occupational or cosmopolitan identity; while as Anthony and Crichton earlier observed, the "history of the personnel specialists as a group is the history or a struggle for status to become full members of the management team". But, at the same time, if only as a reflection of the determination to deploy specialist knowledge as a power resource in their internal struggles for acceptance vis-a-vis their managerial colleagues, the willingness to join the institute of Personnel Management in increasing numbers has been a striking phenomenon of recent years. Moreover, although the competing rationales of a "welfarist" and "technicist" character create status ambiguities which are only imperfectly settled on a group or "collegiate" basis, individual personnel specialists may still resolve such dilemmas to their own satisfaction by developing a hierarchy of personal commitments and allegiances.

But in order to establish further the increasingly important role of mangers and employers' organizations in industrial relations, the growth of the personnel function at enterprise level has also been matched by the parallel integration of national employers' associations, which, while still less influential than their trade union counterparts, have carried out a progressively influential role in national level negotiations. To be sure, the absence of systematic research on employers' association makes it difficult to reach definitive to have been of major importance in the nineteenth century and, as Clegg has observed, specific associations can be traced as far back as trade unions. Moreover, their current functions include, pay bargaining, the working week, overtime, holidays and shiftworking; disputes procedures and advisory and other services. Again , individual associations not only remain viable institutions but have recently adopted stricter policies for dealing with recalcitrant members. And, perhaps most suggestive of all, the origins of the Confederation of British Industry are comparatively recent; a phenomenon which again believe conventional wisdom of their virtual eclipse during the twentieth century.

By the same token, if we broaden the scope of our analysis by drawing upon comparative examples, the saliency of employers' associations in contemporary industrial relations systems can be shown to be very marked indeed. Hence, Hugh Clegg, in *Trade Unionsism Under Collective Bargaining*, felt it fitting to ascribe a major causative role to employers' associations in shaping collective bargaining structures and particularly the levels at which negotiations were typically conducted. Thus, as he observed, the concentration of Swedish bargaining in industry and national level could be attributed largely 'to the organization of Swedish employers in industry associations within the SAF with its centralised authority.' Similarly, industry-level bargaining in Britain was originally closely associated with the organization of employers. Again, "the level of bargaining in France and West Germany corresponds with the structure of their employers' associations. Plant bargaining in American manufacturing industry is the result of the absence of employers' associations there, and helps to account for the high degree of control exercised by agreement and procedures specifically designed to meet the circumstances of each plant or company."

In sum, therefore, this evidence would appear to indicate yet again the fundamental significance of employers' and managerial organizations in industrial relations and to reinforce the view that a great deal of contemporary literature is in need of radical revision on this count. indeed, on balance, the data that are available would appear to support the view that, even in Britain, the advance of personnel specialists at enterprise level has been paralleled by an expanding role for employers' associations over the last decade. Rather, therefore, than workplace bargaining being exclusive of industry-wide or national negotiations the two departures would seem to have been contgeminous. Moreover, particularly in conditions of enhanced state involvement, the pressure upon employers to from together in integrated national movements has been particularly acute.

'Human Resources" or 'Resourceful Humans': Future development in the role of the manager in industrial relations

Indeed, looking to the future, it seems more than probable that employer and managerial initiatives will become increasingly significant in the forthcoming years, not least because of a consciously articulated and independently formulated strategy already in progress to move away form industrial relations narrowly conceived towards the broader encompassing notion of responsibility for "human resources" within the enterprise. Instead, therefore, of adopting even the remotest of reactive postures in this context, managerial personnel have undoubtedly been principal architects. Of course, the success or otherwise likely to be enjoyed here will be dependent upon a serious of further existences such as the style in which such ventures are pursued, the power of other principal actors in the system and economic movements. But this in no way invalidates their significance as part of increasingly sophisticated social science-based attempts by mangers to develop entirely new work concepts which are designed radically to alter the underlying conditions which occasion the incidence of industrial conflict in the first place.

But at all event, there are a number of major social changes already gathering momentum which are likely to accelerate in the years ahead. For example, as Thomason has pointed out, there are several discernible and to some extent interconnected modifications in contemporary social and cultural values and notably: (1) the focus in the educational system on free rather than mechanical abilities; (2) the pressure on individual authority which is likely to lead to consensus management; (3) the conditions of dependency of workers continuing to decline; and (4) and emphasis on fairness and justice in industrial relations becoming increasingly pressing. Again, as the same author has argued, the accompanying "changes in the formal organizational or power structure" will occasion a "fundamental re-thinking of the nature of decision-making processes as it relates to man-management". Moreover, the transformations in the personnel role consequent upon such movements are likely to embrace not only the implementation of policies and prescriptions contained in legislation and collective agreements but also the securing of understanding and comprehension to enable people "to form adequate perspectives if their working environment" and the development of a commitment to common and multifunctional tasks in the enterprise.

Of course, in a great many enterprises in the north American context, so-called "human resourcing" has already replaced the titles of personnel and labour management but if this is to be other than a more palatable framework for camouflaging deeper and more persistent sources of labour unrest, than the fundamental canons of a new industrial relations grouped around the notions of "voluntraism", freedom and creativity would seem to be essential. Again, in such a milieu, technological and structural changes would take the form of facilitating rather than constraining new modes of social action; although, to achieve such an objective the more democratic and open concept of " resourceful humans" would appear to be a preferable formulation. Indeed, as Cowan has recently suggested: "Just as we moved from the medieval society to our present industrial society; so shall we gradually more to a post-industrial society. Technology will become increasingly important and will receive more attention. Resourceful humans achieving a greater sense of fulfillment from their total activities will regard `job satisfaction' as only one of their goals and the human resourcing manager of the post-industrial period will see his job in far wider terms than that perceived by the personnel manager today."

Management in industrial relations: A shift of a paradigm?

But even fairly radical prognostications for the future of industrial relations are almost invariably set within a conventional paradigm of personnel or "human resourcing" management. Nevertheless, it has become clear that, over the last decade or so in particular, mangers in all the main functional specialisms within the enterprise have been progressively more conscious of themselves as a distinctive occupational group. Indeed, on one view. such mangers have gradually come to regard themselves as new partners *in* industrial relations facing problems, which, while by no means identifical with those of the rest of the workforce, share a number of common elements vis-a-vis owners, the state and other groups external to the enterprise. This departure, too, has undoubtedly resulted in the formulation of very different demands from the ones which we have analysed so far and have helped to spawn a range of distinctive associations and organizational entities, and the realignment of traditional conceptions of interests and identity.

In the rest of therefore, our attention will focus appropriately on this consequential but still inadequately charted aspect of the manager's role in industrial relations. Hence, in Chapter 10, Simpson identifies the principal causative elements which have produced a favourable terrain for the fashioning of new allegiances and the development of fresh conceptions of the management's function. In this respect, then, the significance of remuneration, increased labour legislation, the challenge for below, bureaucracy and enterprise size, and industrial democracy are all analysed. Nonetheless, there are clearly a number of possible initiatives and reactions to such social movements and these can include the attempts to satisfy different types of goal including professional and career advancement as well as of goal including professional and career advancement as well as remuneration and status. And, at all events, the upshot has been a number of interesting developments in managerial representation including professional associations, internal or 'in house' associations separate professional managerial bodies, together with white-collar, blue-collar and public sector unionisation. Hence, while naturally there remain considerable variations in modes of adaptatopn, the net effect is still to illustrate yet again the fundamental nature of the manager's role in industrial relations and the considerable intricacies and complexities of the emerging study of this phenomenon itself.

Appendix

Industrial relations in the engineering industry

The general scene

Engineering is the least easily defined of all British industries. It is an area of industry primarily concerned with the manufacture of article made of metal and makes use of a common range of basic skills, especially those of shapping, milling, machining and fitting. But the range of its products has no obvious limits, not are the skills it employs confined only to engineering factories.

The problems of determining where engineering begins and endsa are insuperable. On grounds of products one would certainly class the manufacture of machinery of all kinds as engineering. Would it also be right to classify the manufacture of the metal from which that machinery is made as engineering? If not, at what state in its growth into finished articles does it become engineering? At the other end of the scale, at what point in their type development do manufactured articles cease to be engineering? To give examples, do we class the manufacture of iron and steel as engineering. If not, in which industry do we place the production of heavy forgings and pipes? If we think of vehicle manufacture and the making of electrical equipment as engineering ought we to draw the line at perambulators and Bath chairs and at the production of electrical toys?

It is difficult to avoid the conclusion that engineering is, in the product sense, less an industry than a constellaction of industries. At thesame time it is equally clear that, if we so wished, we could label almost all extractive and manufacturing sections of the economy "engineering". Engineering skills enter into coal mining and electircity generating and into chemical manufacture, and there can be few industries which do not rely at some point on theengineering skill of the maintenance craftsman.

The problem of defining the limits of the engineering industry can only be resolved by arbitrary methods. For general purposes, this is usually done by grouping together a number of headings in the Ministry of Labour's standard industrial classification and designating these "engineering". They include at least some headings falling within metal manufacture, most headings concerned with the production of engineering and electrical goods and vehicles, and some from a group of "metal goods not elsewhere specified", with the addition of marine engineering. The result of such a grouping is to set some kind of limits to what might be thought of as general engineering employment, and at least to exclude engineers employed in maintenance or other capacities in industries not normally considered to be engineering, e.g., chemicals, coal mining, electricity supply, Post Office Telephonbes, etc. Defined in this way, it is reasonable to suppose that at the present time, engineering has a total labour force of rather less than 3.4 million workers, and therefore gives employment to about 13.5 per cent of the insured population of the country. It includes some sectors which are public, e.g., government industrial establishments, but the bulk of engineering production is in private hands in about 18,000 establishments ranging from the giant firm to the small shop employing a handful of wqorkers. It is not possible to say exactly what proportion of the labour force is unionized, but a figure of about 54 per cent would not be unreasonable, taking both manual and staff workers into account.

In the private sector of engineering a few of the largest firms, a considerable number of medium size ones, and the vast majority of very small ones are "non-federated". They either negotiate with trade unions direct or. where many smaller firms are concerned avoid the issue of trade union recognition altogether. A very large proportion of all sizeable engineering firms are however, federated to one employer's organization or another for industrial relations purposes. About fifty such organizations cover the field, but the largest and most influential is the engineering employers' federation which is made up of 39 local associations covering substantially the whole of the United Kingdom, and having in membership some 4500 engineering firms employing about 60 oper cent of the total engineering labour force.

The existence of the Engineering Employers' Federation, its overwhelming size, and its importance in the industrial relations of the industry, given engineering a greater unity in such matters than would appear on the surface. For the Federation has been involved in formal collective bargaining relationships with trade unions for more than 65 years, has been associated with most of the general policies and attitudes which engineering employers have adopted, and currently makes agreements which would be recognized as providing minimum wages and conditions foir engineering workers as a whole. The wage settlements it makes nationally with trade unions for some 1.5 million manual and about .5 million staff workers are cmmonly thought to set a pattern for a section of the economy even wider than that of engineering itself.

A similar, though more complex, situation applies on the trade union side. Here the Confederation of shipbuiding and Engineering Unions forms a common ground for all but a handful of unions with very small membership in the industry. almost all of its 34 member organizations have some interest in engineering, either among manual or staff workers. But membership is very unevenly distrbuted beytween unions. The "Big Six" are, for manual workers, the amalgamated Engineering Union, the Transport and

general Workers' Union, the National Union of General and Municipal Workers, the Electrical Trade Union, the Amalgamated aunion of Foundry Workers and the Boilermakers' amalgamation. These unions make up 77 per cent of the affiliated engineering membership of the CSEU and about 84 per cent of trade union membership in engineering as a whole. Four unions with between 30,000 and 50,000 engineering members, the National Society of Metal Mechanics, the National Union of Vehicle Builders, the National Union of Sheet Metal Workers and Coppersmiths and the amalgamated Society of woodworkers, make up a further 9 per cent of the organized manual labour force of the industry, leaving only 7 percent to smaller craft or local societies.

Among engineering unions the AEU, with a total membership in the United Kingdom of about 1 million, inevitably takes pride of place nationally and in most, though by on means all, areas of the country. Within the framework of the Confederation, the AEU customarily takes the lead in national negotiations on wages and conditions of work, though the Foundry Workers perform a similar role on foundry conditions. The leadership of the AEU, both locally and nationally, is usually in the hands of craftmen, but the major proportion of its membership now consists of semiskilled male workers, and since 1942 women members have also been accepted. By contrast, the Transport and General Workers, Union, with rather more than 200,000 engineering members and the National Union of General and Municipal Workers, with about 190,000, normally draw their leadership from non-craftsmen and only have pockets of craft membership in some parts of the country. Since, in the historical development of trade unionism in engineering the AEU and its forerunner the Amalgamated Society of Engineers have long been the focus of traditional attitudes and growth, the CSEU did not become truly representative of engineering workers until the affiliation of the AEU which took place as late as 1947.

The crowth of trade unions and employers' organizations in engineering

The whole complex of employer and trade union organization in engineering today can only be explained in historical terms. On the workers' side, the establishment of grounds and organization for common action has always been a prime problem. Engineering, as it developed in the later eighteenth and in the mineteenth century, was a highly localized affair, growing in widely separated centres in the north, the Midlands and in the London areas; it also tended to be unspecialized by product. In these circumstances it was natural for trade unions also to develop on a localized basis and to be organized primarily by sectional craft societies which established such terms as they could with engineering employers in their immediate areas.

Such craft societies were disnclined towards common action and national direction, but, after its foundation in 1851 the ASE increasingly dominated the engineering scene. By about 1890, the ASE could claim three-quarters of the engineering membership of the whole country and had moved significantly towards the notion of some degree of national organization and policy. But this did not mean that other engineering societies were reconciled to its leadership, nor that the ASE itself was prepared generally to make common cause with other unions. Indeed, it originally refused to have anything to do with the national Federation of Engineering and shipbuilding Trades which was formed in 1891 under the influence of the Boilermakers' society, and had a very fitful relationship with it thereafter.

Carried forward into the present century, the pattern of organization of engineering unions became more, rather than less, confused. Some societies had grown up which took in both skilled and some semi-skilled grades of worker. Sectional societies proper were confined to craftsmen, and though some craftsmen were prepared to encourage the development of trade unionsim among unskilled workers, they were not, in most unions, prepared to accept them into their ranks. It was into this situation that the Workers' Union entered in 1898, and attained a substantial membersgip maong unskilled engineering workers and machinists, and, especially in the Midlands, among skilled workers as well. But other labourers' unions also came into the field, notably the National Amalgamated Union of Labour, founded, also in 1989, as the Tyneside and General Labouers' Union. It was the Workers' Union and the NAUL which, by amalgamation, established the Transport and General Workers' union and the National Union of General and Municipal Workers respectively. Both these unions had substantial membership in the engineering industry by the 1930.

By that time, as a result of amalgamations and dissolutions, the number of engineering unions had been reduced to about 45, some of them of a strictly craft variety, some extending membership over a number of classes of worker, and some with only marginal interests in the industyry. Outside the Federation of Engineering and Ship building Trades stood all the traditional engineering unions of any size; inside, it was principally supported by the Transport and

General Workers' Union and the National Union of General and Municipal Workers. The organization admitted that it was so weak that outside organizations commonly by-passed it in common discussions in the industry.

Since 1936, the federation position of trade unions in engineering has been transformed. In that year the Federation of Engineering and Shipbuilding Trades was reconstituted as the Confederation of Shipbuilding and engineering Unions with an affiliated membership increased from 80,000 to 175,000. By 1939, all the main engineering unions were in membership except the Foundry Workers and the AEU which joined in 1942 and 1947 respectively. In the new constitution the primary purpose of the Confederation was limited to the taking over, administering and negotiating was limited to the taking over, administering and negotiating of national agreements which its affiliated unions held in common with engineering employers; in other respects it was confined to the looser object of co-ordinating union activity in "trade movements", withdrawals of labour, and joint propaganda. for most purposes individual unions were left free to pursue their own policies.

The confideration was not, therefore, designed to make substantial inroads into the sovereign powers of affiliated organizations. After 1947, the entry of the AEU brought it increased authority. More recently its developing tole in making representations to government departments has brought it increasing rewpect. But, true to its original intention, it is still only the mouthpiece of its affiliated unions and has no independent will of its own. Indeed only two changes have been made which have in any way affected its formal position. Both of these took place in 1947 when the Executive Council authorised for the first time the establishment of joint shop stewards works committees in individual engineering establishments, and provided, under minute 741, additional machinery for inter-union co-operation on strike action, particularly that arising at factory level.

Early organizations of engineering employers for industrial relation purposes were localized and usually ephemeral. It was such organizations which came together temporarily to enforce a widespread lock-out of engineering workers in 1852. Local associations of a more permanent character began to emerge in the 1860's. Of these the Clyde shiphuilders' and engineers' association has become the best known because of a major lock-out of trade unions which it instituted in 1866. Early associations tended to be confined to Scotland, the north-east coast and to Manchester.

From the early 1870's, similar bodies began to appear in other parts of the country, for example, in Liverpol, Sheffield, Bolton and Derby. Such associations were loosely organized for the most part. Joint working arrangements were rare, though some became linked in the "General Association of Master Engineers, Shipbuilders, Machinists, Founders and other Kindred Trades" (usually known as the Iron Trade Employers' Association), which was formed in April 1872 on the initiative of the north-east coast employers for "mutual protection against the actions of trade unions".

The Iron Trades Employers' Association was wound up in 1900, but not before it has been overtaken by the growth of a more comprehensive and powerful organization, the Employers' Federation of Engeering Associations. This was established in 1896 as a result of a joint resolution from employers on the Clyde, the north-east coast and in Barrow and Belfast, but within four years it provided common ground for no fewer than 39 local associations in all parts of the country. By the end of the first world war, which gave a great fillip to representative organizations of all kinds, very few associations of any size or importance remained unfederated. Apart from employers' associations catering for specialized, and often local, sections of the industry and from the Welsh engineers' and founders'which co-exist with a federated to the present engineering employers federation now dominate the engineering field.

Inevitably, the product limits of federated firms are very wide indeed. About a third of the labour force employed is in general engineering, rather more than a quarter in vehicles and aircraft, and one-sixth in electrical engeineering and instruments. Over the course of time, shipbuilding proper has become primarily asociated with the separate shipbuilding employers' federation but marine engineering remains principally with the engineers. The remaining federated labour force is scattered widely over allied trades and plastics, amchine tools, textile and agricultural machinery, foundries of all kinds, boilermaking, tank and drum manufacture, constructional engineering, scale and lift making, and many other sections.

The system of industrial relations in engineering.

It is characteristic of the organizations of all parties to the engineering system of industrial relations that they originated in a scattered and local fashion and have only evolved on a national scale under pressure of events. Even today they are only organized to undertake national action in limited ways. Local employers' associations, conscious that it was they which preceded and formed the national federation, are substantially independent of it. Trade union members, though they have acceded to an increasing amount of national organization and negotiation, still think of their unions as independent entities operating primarily on a local basis and consider themselves free, within the framework provided by national arrangements, to pursue their own immediate interests without too much consideration for outside effcts, It is significant of the attitudes of both sides that no unified and agreed *Handbook of national agreements* was isued until 1949.

Indeed, even a sketch of industrial relations in engineering which emphasizes their local nature distorts the situation. For the bulk of relationship in the industry are *domestic*. They take place, designedly, between trade union representatives and managements in individual establishments. From the 1870's until the first world war it seemed that the situation might develop otherwise. The growth of local associations sugested that industrial relations in the industry might normally be made subject to *district* regulation and settlement, and that this would replace a substantial part of the purely domestic arrangements which preceded it. It was the war itself, and the attitude which employers subsequently took in doscouraging competitiving district wage movements, which virtually destroyed the district patterns of relationship which had previously existed. though vestiges of these still appear in the acceptance of district rats and in the continued existence of some local agreements. If, by 1939, there had been any doubt that industrial relations in engineering would, despite the growth of national agrteements, be primarily domestic, this was removed by the growth in numbers of shop stewards, both during the war and after. The appointment of such stewards had been authorizaed in national agreement as early as 1917-19, but it was not until a quarter of a century later than economic circumstances made their role really effective.

Engineering is notable in that collective arrangements between engineering unions and managements have not, as in many industries, encouraged workers and managements to accept the feeling that their relationships should be regulated substantially by rules laid dowm outside the factory. This phenomenon can be explained in a number of ways.

The main reason is that thecircumstances of engineering production do not readily lend themselves to the notion of outside regulation. It is relatively easy to lay emphasis on this in industries where a fairly uniform product or service is involved , and in which methods and conditions of production vary relatively little from one unit to another. The cotton industry, boots and shoes, and the public utilities are cases in point. But engineering establishments have always been notable, not for similarities in their products, methods and conditions, but for the immense diversity which exists between them, a diversity which is based on fundamental differences in market requirements, circumstances and techniques.

It has always been quite understanable that engineers have thought of domestical industrial relationships first, and all other relationships second, and have not striven to tie themselves down to detailed outside agreements. On no subject of collective bargaining in the industry is this more obvious than on wages. While in some industries it has seemed reasonable to impose upon employers detailed wage structures and arrangements about payments by results, the engineering industry has never considered that such an arrangement would either be sensible or practicable. Agreements at national, and to a lessr degree at local level, lay down a basic structure of minima and guarantees which can act as points of references in domestic wage determinations; but they do not seek to impose any rigid pattern. Such matters are in practice considered to be the preserve of domestic bargaining. Similarly, only a framework of mandatory requirements is laid down on conditions of work. The industry has been thought too complex to develop otherwise.

It is this situation which accounts for the emphasis which the industry places on the "Provisions for avoiding disputes", and the relatively small, and in practice quite separate, role which it assigns to the making of non-domestic agreements. The procedure for manual workers now embodied in a slightly amended version of the Procedure Agreement of 1922, is more fundamental for industrial relations in the engineering industry than its structure of national agreements on wages and conditions. For it is this Procedure which provides a means of settling issues which arise in the workshops, the areas in which the bulk of engineering negotiations take place. Procedure is designed to lay the maximum emphasis on the virtues of domestic settlement. It is not designed to encourage the development of regulation of domestic arrangements by outside agreement. Moreover, in the process of evolution it has become substantially separated from the making of such it has become substantially separated from the making of such agreements.

This separation is ensured by a very simple device. All negotiations in engineering, whether they arise from the workplace of outside it, are *ad hoc*. The industry has not standing a joint negotiation committees of trade unions and employers which meet regularly. When the parties meet, they do so for particular purposes and their mandate is only to resolve issue in hand.

If an issue arises in the workshop, it is an accepted principle that every attempt should be made to settle it at its point of origin. If this is not possible, the question can be taken to successively higher levels-to Works, Local or Central Conference nationally - in order to achieve a settlement. But at each stage only the point immediately at issue is being discussed. Similarly, if a question arises outside the workshop, whether at national, or nowadays very rarely, at local level, negotiations are also confined to this question only.

No provision is made in engineering for the generalization of issues outside the area in which they originally began. The results of negotiations begun nationally are applied nationally; those negotiations begun locally are applied only in the locality from which they came. Most important, settlements arrived at on domestic questions, at whatever level, are applied domestically only in the workshop from which they originated. There is no question of widening he area of non-domestic regulation by extending settlements on domestic issues to employers generally either on a local or national basis.

An understanding of this situations is fundamental to an appreciation of the engineering system of industrial relations. It consists primarily of machinery for handling grievances raised from the shop floor of federated firms. National agreements on wages and conditions are made by separate *ad hoc* meetings between the parties. The aim of the system is to achieve smooth workplace relations by a process of conciliation, and to do this within a framework of national agreements. But it is not the aim of the system to bind the workplace more and more firmly to the terms of outside agreements, since procedural settlements are not taken to constitute precedents for application to all employers.

Within the operation of Procedure itself, there are other characteristics which are peculiar to engineering. True to the principle of avoiding joint bodies, the parties do not think of themselves as negotiating *around* a table, but of negotiating *across* it. More important, it is taken as normal that the device of "employer conciliation" should be used. Grievances arising are taken by trade unions to panels of employers at Local and Central Conference level. These panels have the dual responsibility,both of representing the member firm involved, and of conciliating between the firm and the trade union or unions concerned. Engineering carries with it the trade union or unions concerned. Engineering carries with it the air of an industry in which employers act as judge and jury in their own cause on matters in procedure. In addition, the use of outside arbitrators is avoided, both in procedure and in the making of agreements.

In view of the unusual emphasis it places on domestic relationship, its separation of procedural arrangements from the making of agreements and the uncommon characteristics of its procedural machinery, it is not surprising that th engineering system of industrial relations has often been subject to criticism. Whether such criticisms are well founded or not is a question taken up i the final chapter of this book For present purposes it is sufficient to suggest that, whatever its strengths and weaknesses, the engineering system has evolved to meet the peculiar needs of the industry. Looked at in terms of the growth of engineering and of the problems which have arisen in it, the logic of such a system is readily apparent.

The evolution of the engineering system

No formal national framework of industrial relationships in the industry existed before the conclusion of the *Terms of Settlement* of 1898. The early development of craft unionism implied nothing more than local attempts by unions to protect the interests of the craft by imposing such terms upon individual employers as they could secure by using pressures of scarcity of craftsmen and selective strike action in engineering workshops. Unions themselves had no great interest in developing any general framework of relationships with employers; nor were they interested primarily in negotiation as such, nor in negotiating procedures. They were much more concerned to impose upon them such craft conditions as they thought necessary for the protection of craft rights and status.

It is not surprising that engineering employers came to regard craft union claims as a challenge, and threat they felt themselves compelled to "contain" this challenge, first by common organization and later by adding to this a structure of relationships between the parties. For the claims of the unions were simple but fundamental. Firms were to pay the union rate; they were to accept that the unions should control the supply of skilled labour through limitations of numbers of apprentices; they were to concede that unions had the right to establish when piecework should be introduced, to determine what grade of worker should be employed upon a machine and, in the interests of equity between workers, what overtime should be worked.

Had the industry been less liable to technical change and more limited in its products and production methods, engineering employers might not have felt compelled to issue so strong a challenge to these policies of the unions. But in the nineteenth century, as now, engineering was subject to periods of rapid technological and market changes which both encouraged craft union attempts to obtain security for their members by "craft control" and encouraged employers to put up stiff resistance, sometimes individually, sometimes locally, and sometimes nationally.

The earliest large scale conflict took place in 1852, when a temporary but powerful "Central Association of Employers and Operative Engineers" enforced a widespread lock-out in resistance to union demands to restrict overtime, piecework and the use of laborers on machines. The lock-out was successful. Though it by no means removed demands for craft control, it had the effect of moderating trade union militancy and, during the period of relative stability and steady growth in trade which followed, to ensure a period of relative peace in the industry.

The peaceful relations which characterized the 1860's, 1870's and 1880's were also promoted by the increasing willingness of unions to negotiate, rather than to attempt to impose, district minimum rates, and by the tendency of trade union leaders to encourage the development of *ad hoc* conferences with employers locally to settle issues in dispute. For a time it seemed that a new and more sympathetic understanding had arisen between trade unions and employers. But such an understanding, if it ever existed, failed to stand up to the worsening economic conditions of the later 1880's and early 1890's and to the growth of at new trade union militancy. By 1892, the local struggles taking place over issues of craft control were as violent as ever. Engineering workers saw no other way of protecting their interests than by asserting their opposition to piecework, overtime, and to pressures to accept increasing numbers of semi-skilled operatives when these practices appeared to menace their employment prospects.

Engineering employers, confronted by the new militancy and already worried by German and American competition, considered that they had no alternative but to resist the unions' claims in their entirety. On 13 July 1897, following widespread strike threats, the newly formed Employers' Federation enforced its counter-threat to lock out the militants and the unions withdrew their members from federated firms.

The dispute lasted 30 weeks; the unions were defeated. In negotiations to find the basis of a settlement during November and December 1897, the responsibility fell mainly upon the employers to propose a structure e of relationships which would restore peace to the industry and provide a lasting framework of institutions for the future. The *Terms of Settlement of Settlement* of January 1898 were the result.

the choice of s available to the negotiators was in practice limited. The possibility of setting up Joint Boards was discussed. Such a development would have brought engineering into line with many other industries and would have commonly been thought a progressive solution. Some trade union leaders favoured it, but were conscious that their members did not. Though such Boards had been tried in engineering in some parts of the country there was a general fear among trade unionists that employers might seek negotiations on the restrictive rules and regulations upon which craft security was based, and that agreements might limit their freedom of manoeuvre.

Employers were also generally unwilling to accept the Joint Board solution. Their primary interest lay in preserving for themselves, in the rapidly changing market and technical circumstances of the industry, as much freedom as possible from trade union craft control. Joint Boards, they fears, would "practically control the management of the employers' works". The burden of their thinking lay on "Managerial Functions"-on the right of managements to run their establishments as they though bests.

Given the rejection of Joint Boards, the problem of devising a viable structure of relationships between the parties still remained. The employers were willing to concede the principle of recognition of, and negotiations with, trade unions, but they also wished to resist the demands of craft control and assert their managerial functions. The answer was found in the now familiar device of using both *ad hoc* negotiations and Provisions for the Avoidance of Disputes.

The employers undertook to accept collective bargaining and to negotiate general alterations in wages in any district with trade unions through their local association; at district level they undertook, again through their associations, to discuss any question which trade unions wished to raise. *Outside* the factory, engineering was to be regulated by *ad host* agreement.

Inside the factory the situation was to be different. The employers declared that they "would admit no interference with the management of their business, and reserve to themselves the right to introduce into any federated workshop, at the option of the employer concerned, any condition of labour under which any members of the trade unions..... were working at the commencement of the dispute. However, any workmen involved in domestic disagreements with their employers were to be free to refer the matter to their trade union officials, who could raise it with the local employers' association, and failing agreement, with the Executive Board of the Employers' Federation. Meanwhile there was to be "no stoppage of work, either of a partial or general character, but work shall proceed meantime under the current conditions."

The form in which this machinery was conceived explains why the engineering tradition has been one of "employer conciliation" and absence of arbitration. The employers thought tha it was of fundamental importance that, at each procedural stage, they should, individually or collectively, be free to resist any domestic claim or any district demand which they though to be unreasonable, or contrary to their managerial interests. If these interests, and on the trade union side, the interests of the craft, could not be regulated by Joint Boards, no more could they be judged by outside conciliators and even less by arbitrators required to issue awards of a binding character.

The effect of the 1898 *Settlement* was to accept collective bargaining while at the same time providing a structure of relationships in which managements could assert the maximum freedom for themselves in the workshop, with the knowledge that a procedural safety valve had been provided in case of domestic disputes. If it was not possible to eliminate the demands of trade unions in control of machine manning, overtime and the introduction of piecework, it was possible to *contain* them, while at the same time ackonwledging union negotiating rights.

The determination of engineering employers has made these basic features of collective relationships permanent. Their permanence was confirmed in 1922, when, alleging that the Amalgamated Engineering Union was attempting to assert control of overtime, the employers once again located out the unions and restated the position even more clearly in the 1922 Manual Workers' Procedure Agreement substantially in force today.

It is true that the district agreements which were originally envisaged in 1898 have almost entirely been transferred to national level. It is true that some significant exceptions to managerial functions in the workplace have been introduced, and that the development of shop steward organization has, in at least 60 per cent of federated firms, formalized and extended the working of domestic grievance procedure into domestic negotiations. But in all its essentials, the system devised in 1898 still formally survives.

The purpose of this book is to examine th

current working of the system and to encourage trade unionists, managers and students of industrial relations to discuss its strengths and weaknesses. But it is relevant to return at this stage to the fundamental character of the engineering industry itself. The area which, for industrial relations purposes, we call engineering is merely a convention held together only by historical attitudes, by a common procedure, and by a framework of national agreements between the engineering unions and the Engineering Employer's Federation. The span of its product markets, the variety of its techniques of production and domestic practices has not diminished over the past century; diversity has increased with each succeeding year. While the nineteenth century clamour over craft control and managerial functions which was so compelling a factor in the original structure has become muted the more fundamental problem still remains. It is the problem of organizing the industrial relations of an industry which is not, in any of the usually acceptable senses, an industry at all, and in which flexibility of domestic arrangements has always seemed fundamental to economic growth and progress.

9 Industrial Training

Those responsible for training in companies often regard their work as vulnerable. If times are hard, then training programmes are among the first to suffer cutback. It was partly to change this situation that we had the 1964 Industrial Training Act to boost the provision of training on companies. That intervention was only temporarily successful and the more rigorous circumstances of recent years have shifted governmental priorities in the UK towards provision for the unemployed, and companies are less constrained by the requirements of industrial training boards.

Company training budgets remain vulnerable because training is often regarded as an optional extra: 'without proper training we may not be here in five years, but without more productivity and cash in the bank we won't be here next week'. Sadly some training programmes are indeed expendable because they are not geared to real organizational needs and are of dubious effectiveness. The purpose of this chapter is to make a case for training and then to review some methods of putting it into practice.

The need for training in companies.

The advantages of training range from more effective use of resources to considerations of the overall purpose of the enterprise.

Resources

The people in an organisation are its major resource. If they are not appropriately trained for the work they have to perform they will not do it as efficiently as they could and operations will not be as profitable as they might be. Some degree of investment in training can make the human resources at the disposal of the management more productive and more profitable.

Fragmentation of work

Specialisation is growing so that the work to be done within the undertaking is constantly being broken up into smaller parcels. New departments are set up to specialise in a particular aspect of the company's affairs, and each employees people to work in a specialised rather than in a general field. In the management ranks this produces the functional specialist who can do one or two things well, replacing the gifted amateur who could do many things with reasonable competence. This means that each employee needs training to undertake his duties, and this need is likely to become grater.

New skills and knowledge

One consequence of specialisation is obsolescence in skills and knowledge. Many people in the financial and administrative field, for example, have forced themselves through the traumatic experience of accepting electronic data processing in the last decade. The acceptance has made it necessary for them to take some training so that they understand the monsters that are spewing forth information at such an alarming rate. The arrival of the computer has rendered obsolete some of the established administrative skills. This effect of technological development is apparent in every part of commercial and industrial activity. Few if any people will still be practising at forty the skills they learned at twenty. The new skills have to be taught.

It is short-sighted, expensive and impractical merely to hire new people who happen to have picked up the new skills elsewhere. The challenge of retraining the adult has to be faced, both by the employer and by the individual concerned. With managerial staff especially, there is the even more demanding need constantly to develop new understanding of the environment in which the organisation is functioning. Changes in law, economic circumstances and in the community outside the organisation have great influence on affairs within the organisation, and knowledge of the environment is essential to managers.

On the job training

Some people counter this sort of argument by saying that training should take place outside the field of employment, and that the substantial proportion of the gross national product channeled into further education should take care of industrial training needs by training people in colleges and government training centres in the whole span of skills and areas of knowledge that are developing. Those who make this point would usually be surprised by the extent of what is done in this way, but still the training that is done off the job cannot be completed off the job. Just as a person learning to drive has to sit in the driving seat and drive along the street during his training, so the apprentice engineer, the trainee typist, laboratory technician, supervisor, personnel officer, sales manager and other industrial trainees all have to get their academic training in practical perspective, which is best done in the working situation. Also much necessary training is in routines which are peculiar to one company, so that although a supervisor may learn much of great value on a supervisor's course at the local college it will be equally important for him to learn his own company's disciplinary procedures, and this can obviously come only form an agent of the employer.

Employee expectation

There is a standard of expectation which prospective employees have about what the company provides for its recruits. They will expect canteen facilities and locker rooms. Many will expect pension provision and sick pay. If these basic expectations are not met, they will not come and work for the company unless they have no choice, or unless they are likely to earn much more money than they would elsewhere, More and more employees are expecting to receive systematic training for the job when they join a new company rather than having to 'sit next to

Nellie.' A well-run training scheme will be an aid to recruitment. Complete lack of training will be a disincentive to prospective recruits.

Social purpose

All administrators and managers have a view of the purpose of their enterprise that goes beyond mere survival and profitability. One of management's many objectives is that the company should be a place worth working in, and that the people working there can to some extent achieve personal fulfillment. Assuming that a company has a personnel policy which recognises its employees as people rather than simply resources, then the requirements for industrial training are the requirements of the people employed as well as the requirements of the employer.

Administering the training function

The passing of the Industrial Training Act led to many companies taking the concept of specialisation too far, and training departments were set up where the managers reported directly to the managing director or to the general manager quite independently of the personnel department. The reason for this manager quite independently of the personnel department. The reason for this was usually the calibre of the uncumbent personnel manager, or the alarm of the managing director at the prospect of being 'fined' by his industrial training board for not meeting their requirements. In the mid 1960s many personnel managers were limited in their thinking to aspects of employee welfare such as canteen lavatories and record-keeping rather than taking the broader view of personnel which is common today. As a result this type of personnel manager was not considered the appropriate person to be responsible for training with its new levy sanction, and most of the bright, keen training officers who started emerging were not prepared to report to that type of company executive.

This produced a split in the personnel function. Fortunately this practice is now less common except in the largest organisations with substantial training requirements, but it is important to appreciate that personnel work is an amalgam of many activities including training, employment, payment, trade union recognition, discipline, grievances, the design of jobs and consultative arrangements. Each of these interlocks with the others and they have to be co-ordinated and administered under an overall personnel policy. One cannot be isolated from the rest without risks. Effective training depends on effective selection, improved industrial relations often require new training programmes and training innovations frequently influence the industrial relations environment. In considering how the training function is administered, it is therefore of primary importance to see it as part of personnel work.

The personnel function should not usually report to a line manager. If the responsibility for any aspect of personnel comes under, say, the production manager, then managers in marketing, R & D and other areas will regard it as a specifically production function-as may the production manager. It must be seen to be available to, and necessary for, all company functions. Furthermore the responsibility of the training specialist does not interfere with the line authority of the manager. The training officer provides a specialist service to all line managers in the organisation. His particular usefulness lies in his understanding of the requirement of the training board for the relevant industry, his expertise in the skills and the knowledge needed to administer a training programme, his awareness of how people learn, his knowledge of courses and potential visiting lectures. He has a general responsibility for the quality of training provided in the organisation, but the individual line manager remains responsible for the performance and competence of his own staff. The line manager needs to a appreciate what the training function can do for him in developing that competence: he cannot wash his hands of the responsibility and 'leave it to personnel'. They can only provide him with some services that he has to understand and use.

Integration with other functions

Responsibility for specialist training services needs to be integrated with the whole of the personnel function, which must in turn be integrated with the management of the enterprise. Personnel and training are actively concerned with ensuring that the organisation meets it business objectives, not some parasitical unnecessary growth imposed by an outside agency.

Objectives

corporate objectives need to be reappraised to consider the place of training within the total personnel activity. What are its objectives? How do these fit in with the existing business objectives? What targets have to be achieved? This procedure sounds obvious, but it is perhaps the aspect of training which is most often ignored, with the consequent vulnerability of the training arrangements.

Identification of training needs

The person responsible for training has first to establish what the training needs of the organisation are. He will consider two aspects of this. First he will investigate the operational efficiency of the organisation. Later he will look at the training needs of individual people, and the need of the organisation for people to be trained. In considering operational efficiency, he will seek to identify those jobs within the organisation that appear to be holding back to the achievement of proper levels of performance and where training may help to lift this level to one that is acceptable. He will take not of the various indicators which personnel people use to 'take the temperature' of working groups.,

Absenteeism, labour turnover, punctuality, sickness, changes in output level, complaints and labour troubles can all be indicators of the stage of morale in a department, and low morale may be caused by inadequate training. There may be data available form work study officers who feel that the work standards in a particular department are not satisfactory. Conversations with managers and supervisors will suggest other areas requiring attention. The training officer's own experience and training will suggest others, as will the officers of the industrial training boards.

The training officer will therefore collect a mass of information about the training needs that exist within the company, and can then begin to draw up proposals about what training should be done and in what order, the priority usually being determined by the likely pay-off. He may suggest, for example, that the training of typists could be altered to enable newly recruited school-leavers to reach an acceptable level of proficiency in half the time now considered as necessary, at a saving of —x a year, followed by specially designed programmes of operator training in selected departments to reduce the level of labour turnover and to boost output. He might suggest middle managers attending courses at a business school, or supervisors having a series of discussions on the implications of recent legislation. Whatever the particular proposals, he will draw these up and require them to be endorsed by his management colleagues or superiors, so that he has a mandate to start work.

Implementation of the training programme

When the training officer has received his mandate he will also be empowered to spend some money to implement his programme. This will be based on his prediction of how much he can produce in the way of operating economies. The expenditure will come broadly under two headings. First there will be expenditure on hardware and fees, which are outgoings that would not be incurred if the training were not done. Hardware can range from boxes of chalk to overhead projectors, teaching machines and fully equipped, soundproof lecture theatres. Fees will be either the fees payable for employees to attend courses, or payable to outside experts to come and take part in internal courses. The training officer, lake any other executive submitting a budget for approval, is likely to ask for more than he needs under this heading, as he expects those who have to sanction his budget to cut it. It may be sensible for a newly established training function to start off with a minimum of equipment and to invest more heavily when experience has been gained. The reason for this is that most training programmes change fundamentally after a spell of running in an the benefits of experience. Heavy initial investment can result in an accumulation of expensive equipment that is unused, and a dearth of equipment that is needed but not available because the budget has been overspent.

The second category of expenditure is salaries and wages of trainees, where the administrator perhaps needs to scrutinies proposals closely. Employees away from work on training courses are still being paid. In the case of most managers and supervisors this adds nothing to the cost of their duties being carried out. Someone else will deputise for them in their absence, they will catch up with their work when they return, and that is that. In some other cases, however, there may be expenditure of either increasing the establishment for a department so that people absent for training can be covered, or arrangements for colleagues to work expensive overtime to make up the shortfall. The training is necessary, but this type of consideration needs to be thought of before the training begins so that the cost implications are fully appreciated.

As well as hardware, the training officer will need some space to run his schemes in. Some training will be done on the job or in a training section of the normal job environment, such as the apprentice bench in an engineering shop. Some training will be carried out away from the premises altogether, as when a young manager goes to the nearby polytechnic to take a management course. But there will be a need for some of the training programme to take place away from the job but on company premises. Typists are often trained in a small school within the company, and a number of short courses may be run to give mangers or others an appreciation of a subject or to give training in certain skills that are needed.

Evaluation for training effectiveness

Finally in setting up a training function, there is a need for some means of evaluating the training, and this is one of the most nebulous and unsatisfactory aspects of the training job. The starting point is to compare the results achieved with the original objectives and, where possible, to measure the degree of improvement. This can be done in such areas as labour and material utilisation, or the reduction in the number of despatch errors being made in a warehouse. It can only be guessed in the more difficult areas such as the quality of supervision by a foreman before and after a training course. This often depends on a subjective assessment that may be influenced by the reactions of the trainee.

Another possible means of evaluation is to measure the benefits that are set as objectives at the beginning of the programme. It might be a drop in labour turnover and other measures of improved efficiency and employee morale. There may be fewer accidents or reduced levels of overtime. It is also important to attempt some evaluation of the intangibles, such as atmosphere in industrial relations, customer satisfaction, self-confidence among managers and so on. To some extent this can be done by the use of an outside adviser who can come along for a day to examine the situation relating to training within the organisation and then report upon it, rather like an auditor.

It is useful from a training point of view to carry out some form of performance appraisal regularly among employees. If this is done systematically over several years, the validity of training arrangements will be confirmed or otherwise.

Training for different categories of employee

Operators

The large single grouping in the employed population is the operator on the shop floor who has no craft skills-the general worker. His job may require such a small amount of skill and knowledge that he needs no training other than a short period of being shown how' by his supervisor. There are, however, very few jobs which genuinely fall into this category. Most would be done better by more satisfied employees if they were preceded by a period of training, which covered induction to the organisation and the place of the job in the manufacturing process, as well as the mechanics of how it should be done.

As operator jobs in manufacturing are usually specific to each employer, the training needs to be set up and run with in the company as there is no outside body either with the understanding of the job or any alternative source of supply of trainees. The training officer will need to study the operations and to use a process of skills analysis to devise a programme of training to be carried out by an instructor instructing trainees Seldom is the training load large enough to justify a full-time instructor, and it is usual for an experienced operator in each department to be trained in instruction so that he does all the instruction needed by new recruits. Another method is for the foreman to be trained so that he inducts and trains all those in his department. This may be the best method as long as the training job is not going to take up too much of this time.

Skills analysis can be learned at one of the many introductory courses for training officers run within the further education system. Alternatively there are short crash courses available. Instructors can be trained by one of the Training within Industry courses provided by the Training Services Division of the Manpower Services Commission.

Clerical

Very little training is provided in clerical duties in most orgnisations, although the provision of training is spreading and companies find that it pays big dividends in cost savings and employee satisfaction. The practice of clerical training is similar to that for operator training, although there are certain more general occupational skills involved, so that the further education system is more helpful. Widely available is a course in office skills which is taken by young people on leaving school. They attend technical college for one day a week and learn simple office skills and routines to fit in with the working experience they are beginning to acquire. There are also many courses in short-hand and typing, although the demand for shorthand is declining and the school-leaver with reasonable GCE 'O' level achievement can take courses in business studies on day release.

Craft

Once of the first areas to repay attention is the training of craft apprentices, as this is a long and expensive business. Some of the training boards gave the largest amount of their attention of their attention to this area in the first few years of their operation.

Apprentices are recruited at the age of sixteen on leaving school and serve an apprenticeship of several years before being accepted as craftsmen at the end of their training, usually at the age of twenty-one or twenty-two. Most apprentices are young men, although young women do follow apprenticeships as well, but these are heavily concentrated in hairdressing. Many companies follow the customary practice of binding apprentices by indentures, under which the apprentice is obliged to stay with the employer until finishing his 'time' and the employer agrees to provide his training.

A major part of the apprentice's time is spent in further education at a local college, learning the theoretical background of his craft and some manual skills. While with the employer, he needs to practice the skills he is learning and to develop them by applying his knowledge and ability to a growing range of work. Traditionally this has been done by watching, helping and copying a craftsman at work. Gradually this method is being replaced by systematic and full-time training under an instructor in charge of a group of apprentices.

If an organisation is not big enough to warrant the services of a full-time instructor, it is often possible to join a group training scheme, in which a number of small and medium-sized companies pool resources to employ a training officer who organises the training of the apprentices in all the companies. In return, the individual company pays a relatively modest fee to the probably moves from one firm to another in the group.

There are usually national agreements between employers and trade unions regarding the employment and training of apprentices.

Technician

A category in which the number of employees is growing is that of technician, who is one step up from a craftsman and is likely to be concerned more with design than with manufacture. In the field of engineering, the fitter is the craftsman and the draftsman is the technician, although there are many others classified as craftsmen and technician, although there are many others classified as craftsmen and technicians respectively in that industry. To some extent the training needs are common, as the basic technology is the same, but the technician's training needs go further. He is likely to have better educational qualifications at the outset and his further education will go to a higher theoretical level. His practical training will tend to lie in conventional white collar rather than manual operations. It is usually carried out in close conjunction with a qualified man.

Technologist

It is difficult to distinguish between technicians ad technologists and in many industries such a distinction cannot be drawn at all. A rough and ready identification would be by the word 'professional'. In engineering, for example the technologist is the professional engineer who has achieved membership of one of the constituent bodies of the Council of Engineering Institutions. This requires a high level of academic qualification together with the appropriate working experience.

In this category will be the ex-technician who has taken the HNC/HND route through day release or evening courses, as well as the technical graduate who starts his working life in his early twenties. These are the people on whom the technical competence and progress of the organisation will depend. The HNC/D method of qualification is in the process of being replaced by the scheme of the Technical Education Council. Courses for technical graduates now have the interesting development of a small number of courses in selected universities that combine engineering and management studies, usually over four years of study.

The man who comes up through the ranks will need facilities to pursue his academic studies, either by day release or by sandwich course. His practical expertise will be acquired almost incidentally as long as he has reasonable opportunities for varied working experience, rather than being classified as a trainee who cannot be given a proper job because he has not finished his education.

The technical graduate who joins industry in

his early twenties with academic qualifications of a high order but no practical experience usually needs some form of graduate apprenticeship while he spends a number of months acquiring the practical experience that is needed to go with his theoretical grounding.

Management

Training managers is a very different matter form training other categories of workers in industry. This is largely because a smaller proportion of the manager's job content can be isolated and taught. To be effective a manager needs to learn management techniques, such as various methods for the quantification of data so that decisions may be soundly based. he also needs knowledge in such areas as the behavioral sciences so that he can understand how employees may react in certain situations, and so that he can understand how employees may react in certain situations, and so that he may plan sensibly for the future. Beyond this, however, there is still a large area of training or development needed for the individual management trainee, so that he acquires the stature and confidence needed for the job of leadership, gains judgement and determination and develops good timing and a sensitive awareness in handling people.

Largely because of the difficulty and lack of definition in the task of management training, most large organisations separate this particular aspect of training and give the responsibility to management development officers within the training function. The body of knowledge and some of the skills can come from the educational system. In addition to the business schools, which cater for a small fraction of the total amount of management training, there are a number of polytechnics and universities with management departments running courses with recognition from some professional body. The most widely recognised management qualification available in the field of further education is the Diploma in Management Studies, run under the auspices of the Department of Education and Science. It is operated at a limited number of centres and provides a broadly based management education for the well qualified entrant with limited practical experience. There are also courses run under the aegis of, for instance, the Institute of Personnel Management and the Institution of Industrial Managers which provide a broad management education with particular emphasis on the specialism that the professional body represents.

In conjunction with further education, the trainee manager will need controlled working experience and career development so that he can apply his developing skills and knowledge. He may also need careful coaching to help him develop qualities such as judgement and timing. All managers need constantly to bring themselves up to data with new techniques or with new constantly to bring themselves up to date with new techniques or with new knowledge. Thus, professional bodies like the British Institute of Management and many firms of professional consultants conduct admirable short courses, running for a few days or a few weeks, to update the experienced manager. Typical of these have been the endless variety of courses and conferences to brief managers on unfair dismissal legislation, safety and health, or negotiating skills. The next chapter deals with management development in more detail.

Supervisory

Training of first-line supervisors is generally unsatisfactory in the United Kingdom, and the foreman has more than once been referred to as the forgotten man of British industry. Much of the problem lies in the uncertainty about the nature of the job. In the early years of this century the foreman was a man of considerable power and authority in factory, with extensive discretion in decision-making, and was often a general manager in all but name, Since then we have seen the professionalisation of management and the development of shop steward authority. The professionalisation of management has spawned countless middle managers who have taken bits of the foreman's job away from him, like the production engineer and the training officer. The development of shop steward authority has largely done away with the foreman's role as representative of shop-floor feeling, and he is constantly bypassed as shop stewards negotiate with middle and senior managers at meetings he is not invited to attend.

As the position of first-line supervisor is so

difficulties to define, training for it presents obvious problems. The most useful approach is probably the in-company course which aims to inform foreman of the changes taking place around them and give them an understanding of company procedures together with an introduction to such vague but necessary subjects as leadership and human relations. An attempt to establish a course for foremen within the further education system has not received widespread support.

Administrative

The term 'administrative' covers an amorphous group f people who are lumped together because their work is neither clerical nor managerial. They are such people as cost accounts, computer programmers and systems analysts, salesmen and O & M staff

For the cost accountant, training will usually be on the job as a cost clerk while he makes his way through the further education courses for cost and management accountants, perhaps after starting with an Ordinary National Diploma in Business Studies while he is making up his mind about the area in which he wishes to specialise.

The training of computer personnel operates at various levels. Most courses in management include some elements of computing, even if only at the appreciation level, and there are a number of degree courses in computation. Computer operators and data input personnel are still mainly trained by computer manufacturers or specialised private agencies.

Shop stewards

The final category is shop steward. It is the joint responsibility of management and trade unions to train shop stewards are provided by the trade unions, and an introductory course for newly elected shop stewards in run at many educational centres under the auspices of the TUC. It is difficult for many employers to provide satisfactory courses of their own, as stewards are likely to be suspicious of them, but this field of training will not doubt develop.

Training methods

Teaching someone to *do* something requires a different approach from teaching someone to *understand* something. This broad distinction between training in skill and training in knowledge has been refined by research in the training field to produce a division of all types of learning into five basic types.

Some learning involves theoretical subject matter, knowing how, why and when certain things happen. This is *comprehension:* examples are the laws of thermodynamics, the currency structure of the EEC, or the arguments justifying the recognition of trade unions. *Reflex* learning is involved when when skilled movements or perceptual capacities have to be acquired, involving practice as well as knowing what to do. Speed is usually important and the trainee needs constant repetition to develop the appropriate synchronisation and co-ordination. Typing is one of the many jobs that requires reflex learning.

Attitude development is concerned with enabling people to alter their attitudes and social skills. *Memory* training is concerned with learning how to cope with varied situation and *procedural* learning is very similar except that the drill to be followed does not have to be memorised, but located and understood. This categorisation produces the mnemonic CRAMP.

Learning for comprehension requires the whole subject to be treated as an entity and the lecture or training manual are appropriate methods. Attitude change is typically handled by group discussion, but reflex learning, is best handled by part methods, which break the task down into sections, each of which can be studied and practised separately before putting together a complete performance. Memory and procedural learning may take place either by whole or part methods, although memorisation is usually done by parts.

Index